Solving Sprawl

Solving Sprawl

*Models of Smart Growth
in Communities Across America*

F. Kaid Benfield
Jutka Terris
Nancy Vorsanger

Natural Resources Defense Council

The Natural Resources Defense Council (NRDC) is a national nonprofit environmental organization with more than 500,000 members. Since 1970, our lawyers, scientists, and other environmental specialists have been working to protect the world's natural resources and improve the quality of the human environment. NRDC has offices in New York City; Washington, D.C.; Los Angeles; and San Francisco.

Book Design and Production Bonnie Greenfield	*Book and Cover Design* Jenkins & Page
NRDC Reports Manager Emily Cousins	*NRDC Director of Communications* Alan Metrick
NRDC President John Adams	*NRDC Executive Director* Frances Beinecke

Cover photographs: The Crossings: Calthorpe Associates. Horse pasture: *Landscapes, Managing Change in Chester County 1996–2000.* Comprehensive Policy Plan Element, 1996. Reprinted with the permission of the Chester County Planning Commission, West Chester, PA. Bethesda Row: Federal Realty.

To order additional copies, send $20.00 each plus shipping and handling ($3.50 for the first book, $1 each additional book). Make checks payable to NRDC in U.S. dollars only and mail to: NRDC Publications Department, 40 West 20th Street, New York, NY 10011. California residents must add 7.25% sales tax. For more information, call 212-727-4486 or visit us at www.nrdc.org.

Library of Congress Cataloging-in-Publication Data
Benfield, F. Kaid.
Solving sprawl : models of smart growth in communities across America / F. Kaid Benfield, Jutka Terris, Nancy Vorsanger.
      p. cm.
Includes bibliographical references.
ISBN 1-893340-33-3
1. City planning-United States—Case studies. 2. Cities and towns—United States—Growth—Case studies. I. Terris, Jutka, 1972- II. Vorsanger, Nancy, 1963- III. Title.
HT167 .B46 2001
307.76'0973--dc21
      2001005025

9 8 7 6 5 4 3 2 1
This book was printed in Canada on 100% recycled paper that is 50% post-consumer waste and processed chlorine free.

Table of Contents

Foreword

The desire to move up the social and economic ladder is a fundamental part of the American dream. However, for more than a half-century, millions of Americans have acted as if moving *out* to the suburbs is the same as moving *up* in life. Rather than stopping to think about how to make our communities better places to live, many of us rushed headlong into the countryside. In our haste to move up and out, we too often took our natural resources for granted. We paid little attention to what was happening to agricultural communities as farms were fragmented by development, or what was happening to forests—and the wildlife that lives in them—when roads and malls tore through them.

Gradually, we are beginning to realize that our growth patterns are destroying our cherished landscapes. On top of its impact on farm and forest lands, low-density, sprawling growth has destroyed the beauty of our communities, made congestion worse, and forced our citizens to pay higher and higher taxes to meet the demand for sprawl-supporting infrastructure.

Finally, we are beginning to realize that we need to rethink the way we grow.

The national smart growth movement emerged out of this realization. Sprawl affects all states and all regions, whether their population is increasing rapidly or not at all, whether they are urban, rural, or somewhere in between.

In Maryland, we looked ahead and saw that, if current growth patterns continued, we would consume as much land with new development in central Maryland alone over the next 20 years as we had in the previous 367 years of our history.

In Georgia, air quality concerns, stemming in part from sprawl-related traffic, led the federal government to suspend financial assistance for new highway construction, and the Atlanta Chamber of Commerce expressed alarm that phenomenal highway congestion was killing the region's economic competitiveness.

In Pennsylvania, 25 percent of the state's rich farmland has been converted to non-farm uses since 1970, and local governments expect the waves of growth coming out from urban areas to continue.

In Utah's greater Wasatch area, beneath the majestic Wasatch Mountains, the population is expected to increase from the current 1.7 million residents to 2.7 million in 2020, creating pressure to develop ecologically sensitive land.

Each state is developing its own solutions to these problems based on its own values, traditions, and geography. But all of the states engaged in this effort to better manage growth share a basic starting point: they do not want to stop growth, or even slow it down. They just want to be smarter about how—and where—we grow. We want to stop subsidizing the kind of haphazard, costly growth that has devoured our country-side and destroyed our quality of life at an alarming rate.

In Maryland, we have developed a two-part strategy of protecting our best remaining open space while simultaneously reinvesting in existing communities. Our smart growth program, among the first in the nation, is incentive-based, not regulatory. It respects the land use authority of local governments, but declares that the state has a legiti-mate interest in how local governments use that authority. In fact, the state's interest is not only a legitimate interest, it is a required and nec-essary interest: it is the state that often must pick up the cost of poor local land-use decisions. As important, states see the large impact of regional traffic congestion and smog, of lost farm and forest land, and of the abandonment of long-established core communities in a way that is often not visible to purely local planning bodies.

In Georgia, Governor Roy Barnes and the Georgia legislature began to address their transportation problems by establishing the Georgia Regional Transportation Authority. This agency has the authority to overrule local transportation, planning, and land use decisions to avoid more sprawl. Surprisingly, the Atlanta Chamber of Commerce was a strong supporter of this effort, as they realized that traffic congestion negatively impacts local businesses.

In Pennsylvania, a yearlong study identified land use as the state's top environmental priority. In response, Governor Tom Ridge and his staff developed the Growing Greener initiative to help with local govern-ments' most pressing infrastructure needs and open space preservation.

In Utah, Governor Leavitt worked with Envision Utah to develop a high-quality growth strategy designed to maintain the state's high quality of life.

Governors, of course, are not the only elected officials grappling with the effects of growth. Local governments are on the front lines in this battle, and they, too, are looking for better ways to grow. This year, the United States' Conference of Mayors and the National Association of Counties have joined the National Governors Association in focusing on growth management and quality of life issues. This is truly becoming a national movement—a movement for positive change.

To some extent, government policies—even well-meaning policies like the tax treatment of home mortgages or the construction of the interstate highway system—got us into this jam. Reversing government policies that encourage sprawl is one way to attack the problem. Another is to demonstrate with bricks and mortar that we can truly be smarter about how we grow.

In many places around the country, these smarter communities are already rising out of the ground. The examples presented here in *Solving Sprawl* demonstrate the variety of problems that these new projects attempt to address, and the innovative solutions that are used. These stories show that the smart growth phenomenon is not limited geographically. Communities hosting smarter developments are urban and suburban, relatively new and truly historic, wealthy and working class. Some of these projects are the brainchild of one innovative risk-taker; others are the result of years of work by partnerships between communities and public, private, and non-profit sectors. As varied as these projects are, they have one thread in common: each improves the quality of life for those who live or visit there.

Smart growth is also about choosing *not* to grow in some places—the open spaces we value for their beauty, agricultural productivity, and ecological function. This book shows how open space preservation can be tailored to the needs and preferences of very different landscapes.

For those of us looking for new and better ways to grow, these stories provide not only best practices to emulate, but inspiration as well. These examples may be even more valuable for friends and colleagues who are not yet convinced that smart growth is anything more lasting than a public policy fad.

Let's face it: in the vast majority of communities, smart growth development—whether a mixed-use neighborhood, a single transit-oriented building, or an infill, reuse, or preservation project—is still the *hardest* thing to do. In the conservative world of land development, it can be difficult to arrange financing for a smart growth project, and even more difficult to gain governmental approval.

Ultimately, the success of the smart growth movement will be judged not by the harmful developments we stop, but by the smarter growth we foster. To overcome the institutional and psychological barriers in our path, we need to develop a record of success. That is why this volume is so important.

Sprawl did not spread overnight. It will not stop overnight. Replacing and retrofitting fifty years of development will take time. But, after reading *Solving Sprawl,* I have faith that, by changing our assumptions and our priorities today, we can shape a better world for tomorrow.

Consider the consequences of two very different visions for the future of America. If we fail, we risk:

- Almost every farm plowed under, and practically every forest paved over

- Destructive traffic congestion spreading and increasing in intensity

- The progress towards a cleaner, healthier environment reversed, with native species again on the decline towards extinction

- Our cities all but abandoned, with houses and businesses boarded-up, like gated communities in reverse where our impoverished citizens are trapped just as surely as if they were imprisoned

- People moving farther out and farther apart, until our sense of community—our very soul—is irretrievably lost

This is a future we cannot accept. It is within our power to prevent it. We can begin by imagining a different future, a better vision that it is within our power to create. It is a future based not just on economic prosperity, but on community prosperity as well. A future where:

- People spend evenings having dinner with their loved ones or at a daughter's soccer game, not sitting in traffic jams

- Vibrant, viable, walkable communities that offer residents a place to work, have dinner, visit a museum, or attend the theater in safety and comfort

- Precious natural resources that are not just protected, but restored for future generations to enjoy

I firmly believe it is time to change our culture, time to adopt a new ethos: We will work hard to sustain our incredible economic growth. We will preserve the beauty of our nation and we will protect our environment. And we will do so through land preservation, quality design, and support for our traditional communities, and solid long-range planning. If we do that, we can improve the quality of life for our citizens now and, more importantly, for our children's children.

Governor Parris N. Glendening
The State House
Annapolis, Maryland
May 2001

Solving Sprawl
with Smart Growth

*Civilization needs an honorable dwelling place, and the
conditions of making that place ought to depend on what
is most honorable in our nature: on love, hope, generosity,
and aspiration.*
                    —James Howard Kunstler, *Home From Nowhere*

James Howard Kunstler's words provide inspiration to those of us
who have been concerned about the American landscape. They
also give us optimism because, when we encounter problems, Americans tend to use the attributes that Kunstler celebrates—love, hope,
generosity, and aspiration—to devise solutions. We have always been
a problem-solving society.

In this book, we shine a spotlight on American communities that
are finding ways to solve the problem of sprawl—the all-too-familiar
haphazard development pat-
tern that has come to dominate our national landscape
from sea to shining sea.
And the results, though only
a beginning, show wonder-
ful promise—if the early
models of smart growth are
replicated—for our environment, economy, and social
fabric. Instead of obliterating our countryside while
jeopardizing our financial
reserves and weakening our

A working farm in a
preserved zone in
Pennsylvania.

social bonds, we are learning how to develop and grow in ways that better reflect our values. It's about time.

In a way, this book is an anomaly. At the beginning of the twenty-first century, it is an unfortunate truth that Americans concerned about the environment seldom have much in the way of progress to enjoy. Global warming, energy shortages, air and water pollution, habitat loss, a continuously spoiled landscape, and other serious problems continue to plague our society, in many cases with trends that portend worsening consequences for the future. As we documented in our 1999 book *Once There Were Greenfields,* many of these serious problems are directly related to suburban sprawl and the way that we have allowed our cities and regions to grow.

As we also noted in *Once There Were Greenfields,* however, it doesn't have to be this way. There is hope, and its name is "smart growth," an approach to developing cities, suburbs, and metropolitan regions in ways that allow us to thrive environmentally, economically, and socially while still providing all the assets of the American Dream and conserving our landscape. In short, smart growth solves sprawl.

What is smart growth? There is no single answer, of course. But one excellent articulation comes from our partners and friends at the Smart Growth Network, an association of businesses, government agencies, and nonprofit organizations committed to promoting alternatives to sprawl: "In general, smart growth invests time, attention, and resources in restoring community and vitality to center cities and older suburbs. New smart growth is more town-centered, is transit- and pedestrian-oriented, and has a greater mix of housing, commercial, and retail uses. It also preserves open space and many other environmental amenities." The network goes on to observe that successful communities "tend to have one thing in common—a vision of where they want to go and of what things they value in their community."

In this book, we use working examples to illustrate these concepts, and to

Smart student housing in California.

Sprawl's rapid land consumption cannot be explained away by population growth only

▶ Between 1960 and 1990, the amount of developed land in metro areas more than doubled, while the population grew by less than half.

Sprawl creates automobile dependence and longer driving distances

▶ Total vehicle use more than tripled between 1960 and 1995 to more than 2.4 trillion miles per year.

▶ Despite technological improvements, highway vehicles are still responsible for about 60 percent of total carbon monoxide emissions in the United States, 30 percent of the chemicals that cause urban smog, and 50 percent of carcinogenic and toxic air pollutants. Transportation contributes 32 percent of total U.S. emissions of carbon dioxide, the most prevalent greenhouse gas.

Sprawl irrevocably damages natural resources

▶ Runoff from new residential development is 10 times that of predevelopment conditions and runoff from commercial development is as much as 18 times higher. Runoff pollution is now the nation's leading threat to water quality.

▶ Sprawl leads to habitat loss, fragmentation, and even the extinction of species. Of 20,000 species of native U.S. plants and animals, fully a third are "of conservation concern": extinct, imperiled, or vulnerable.

▶ Between 1982 and 1992, the United States lost an average of 400,000 acres of "prime" farmland (the land with the best soils and climate for growing crops) to development every year.[1]

tell the story of how smart growth has caught hold in America. We report the good news that smart-growth developments can now be found all across our country, in cities small and large, suburbs old and new. We show that communities embrace these smart-growth neighborhoods, people choose to live and work in them, governments support them and, yes, developers can make money on them. We provide examples demonstrating that, at the same time that we are reinvesting in existing communities and building new ones in smarter ways, we are also strategically saving valuable countryside from the threat of inappropriate development. We bring the good news that communities are implementing a wide array of smart-growth solutions on the ground, and the solutions are working.

Our book also celebrates the American heroes who are leading the way in solving sprawl. We celebrate political leaders, like Governor

There is no single template, no one-size-fits-all definition of how to solve sprawl, of what makes a community or a development "smart." Instead, the features that distinguish smart growth from sprawl vary from place to place. The Smart Growth Network has developed a set of ten basic principles that can be applied in various combinations to create smart, nonsprawling communities:

▶ Mix land uses
▶ Take advantage of compact neighborhood design
▶ Create housing opportunities and choices
▶ Create walkable communities
▶ Foster distinctive, attractive communities with a strong sense of place
▶ Preserve open space, farmland, natural beauty, and critical environmental areas
▶ Strengthen and direct development toward existing communities
▶ Provide a variety of transportation choices
▶ Make development decisions predictable, fair, and cost-effective
▶ Encourage community and stakeholder collaboration in development decisions

Glendening, who has honored this book with his eloquent foreword and who is often credited with popularizing the phrase "smart growth" while infusing it in his state's basic philosophy of how to develop. We feature enlightened corporations, like Adidas, who are choosing to redevelop abandoned city properties rather than build still more automobile-dependent "campuses" in the countryside. We honor bold developers, like Atlanta's Post Properties, who are putting their money and ideas behind new smart-growth communities. We showcase faith-based organizations, like Chicago's Bethel New Life, that have been instrumental in redeveloping inner-city neighborhoods.

We also celebrate creative local officials, like Ken Montlack of Cleveland Heights, Ohio, who are demonstrating that municipalities can work together to preserve and strengthen older suburbs. We honor visionary architects and planners, like California's Peter Calthorpe and Miami's Andres Duany, who are showing how to design communities and regions that solve sprawl. And we feature the work of alert and energetic citizens, like Barry Harper of Almira Township, Michigan, whose organization Save Pearl Lake lived up to its name. We cannot stress enough that these heroes, as well as the others whose stories we tell in this book, and the many more who are working on solving sprawl, are doing so with great creativity and ingenuity.

This book details 35 diverse smart-growth stories from around the country. We have organized our examples according to their locations: first, we introduce a diversity of smart-growth development and redevelopment projects in cities; second, we highlight examples of smart-growth successes in the suburbs; and third, we concentrate on forest, farm, and landscape conservation in places where development is not appropriate.

Within each of these chapters, we strive to show a wide variety of solutions to sprawl, to include projects of all sizes, and to have geographic diversity—to present many different and colorful pieces of the smart-growth mosaic. Interspersed throughout these principal stories, we include sidebars featuring additional examples of smart growth and reminders of the sprawl-related environmental and social problems that smart growth helps us overcome. We have also provided a glossary at the end of the book that may assist readers in learning more about planning terms and land-use concepts that might be unfamiliar.

SNAPSHOT: **AMERICANS SUPPORT SMART GROWTH**

Polls show that Americans strongly support smart growth and the strategies necessary to implement it. Indeed, 78 percent of voters believe that it is important for the U.S. Congress to help communities solve problems associated with urban growth, according to the Millennium Planning Survey, a comprehensive telephone survey conducted by the American Planning Association in October 2000. Another poll, conducted in September 2000 by Smart Growth America, a coalition of over 60 public interest groups, found a similarly high level of support: more than three-quarters of those surveyed said they favored "giving priority to improving services, such as schools, roads, affordable housing and public transportation in existing communities rather than encouraging new housing and commercial development and new highways in the countryside."

Respondents of the SGA poll also overwhelmingly supported a number of specific government policies related to smart growth, including giving priority to funding services in existing communities rather than encouraging new development in the countryside; creating zones for green space, farming, and forests outside existing cities that are off limits to developers; requiring that affordable housing be included in all new developments; and giving funding priority to public transportation over new highways.

Car-dependent commercial sprawl in Virginia.

Some may find it surprising that an environmental organization would place as much emphasis on "brick and mortar" smart-growth developments as on the preservation of natural areas. But a basic underpinning of smart growth is the acceptance that growth is inevitable; after all, in the first half of the twenty-first century, the U.S. population is expected to grow by half, adding some 140 million people who will need housing and places to work, shop, attend school, and relax. It is critical that, in order to keep "dumb growth" out of our most precious wilderness and rural areas—to solve sprawl—we must embrace growth somewhere else.

For the most part, we have chosen not to write about policies and plans—however enlightened—that have not yet materialized. The developments we highlight are already partially or fully built, and many are occupied. The natural areas we feature are already enjoying protection. These developments and protected green spaces can inspire us with their tried-and-true solutions; even their imperfections, which we also discuss occasionally, provide valuable lessons about what works and what doesn't in the real world of solving sprawl.

Our hope is that the reader will come away from *Solving Sprawl* with a renewed sense of hope and inspiration about smart growth, although not with a false sense of complacency. Indeed, as Governor Glendening's foreword reminds us, the status quo is still suburban sprawl, not smart growth. We will need years of hard work to change our policies to make smart growth easier; for developers to try different solutions; for elected officials to take a long-term view; for planners and other public servants to think "outside the box"; and for citizen activists to be planning ahead for growth, not just opposing developments. As a nation, we must become more ambitious. We must not accept blindly the limited choices that have been presented to us in the past. To solve sprawl, we must pursue our dreams for better places to live.

Smart Cities

Lively, diverse, intense cities contain the seeds of their own regeneration, with energy enough to carry over for problems and needs outside themselves.
    —Jane Jacobs, *The Death and Life of Great American Cities*

Jane Jacobs wrote these optimistic words in 1961, a difficult time even for the greatest American cities. Suburban flight was in full swing, having started in earnest at the end of World War II, taking people, jobs, and wealth out of cities into newly built subdivisions at or beyond the urban edge. The new interstate highway system had already started slicing through cities, causing displacement, neighborhood fragmentation, and pollution. Well-intended but disastrous urban-renewal planning policies in the fifties and sixties included "slum clearance" in vibrant, though low-income and often minority neighborhoods, and created isolated pockets of housing projects for the very poor. Historic structures were razed and replaced by buildings lacking character and neighborhood connection. The cumulative effects have lingered for decades.

Yet Jane Jacobs was right in putting her faith in cities. Today, American cities are making a comeback, many with an explicit smart-growth agenda.

For instance, cities are enjoying new economic vigor. Between 1992 and 1997, as many as 2.3 million new private jobs were created in cities—an increase of 8.5 percent, according to *The State of the Cities 2000* report from the U.S. Department of Housing and Urban Development (HUD). Wage growth and overall household income in cities now outpace those of suburbs.

As a result, after years of population loss, U.S. cities are now stabilizing or even growing. Weary of suburban traffic jams, residents and businesses are placing a high value on the easier access to jobs, every-day shopping, and entertainment provided in traditional city neighborhoods with varied transportation options. People of all generations are attracted by the vibrancy and unmatched combination of culture, entertainment, and commerce that cities can offer. Even a growing number of families who previously would have avoided the city are finding ways to embrace a more urban lifestyle.

Although the real estate sector (and especially the financial markets that support it) is traditionally slow to change, there is now increasing recognition that innovative new urban developments can be profitable for investors. PriceWaterhouseCoopers and Lend Lease Real Estate Investments, financial research firms that assess the commercial real estate market each year, named large cities with round-the-clock activities the best investment markets in the 2000 edition of their publication *Emerging Trends in Real Estate*. In fact, while city projects can be slower and more complicated to build than suburban subdivisions and strip malls, their financial returns can be substantial, as some of the stories in this chapter illustrate. Sophisticated public/private partnerships are also on the rise, helping to create projects that the private market alone could or would not build.

To the extent that redevelopment and new "infill" development (see Glossary) on vacant urban land can attract additional residents and businesses, smart cities can strengthen their tax bases while reducing the pressure to develop more sprawl on the fringe of existing suburbs. The examples in this chapter illustrate the great diversity of successful urban development projects, all reflecting principles of smart growth.

Living, Working, Playing in the City

One of the most important features of today's urban renaissance is the rebuilding of city neighborhoods with a mixture of housing, offices, green spaces, entertainment, and civic uses, combining together to make forgotten communities once again convenient and vibrant. In this chapter, we feature a particularly good example in Dallas Uptown, a long-neglected neighborhood north of Dallas's central business district that was rebuilt by a public/private partnership. Another featured example is Atlantic Station, a compact, mixed-use development built on an abandoned industrial site in central Atlanta.

The MCI Center in downtown Washington, D.C. shows that even sports arenas can be part of the smart-growth movement. The MCI Center is unique among several new state-of-the-art sports arenas around the country: it also contains a museum, shops, and restaurants, and it sits right on top of a central mass-transit hub. Situated where three Metrorail subway lines and several bus lines intersect, the arena has not only lured sports fans out of their cars but also catalyzed the surrounding area's revitalization.

Very different from Washington, Dallas, and Atlanta, Suisun City, California, is a smaller city bypassed by a major highway and economic development. However, it also found value in pursuing large-scale, mixed-use development. In fact, by revitalizing its waterfront and historic downtown, Suisun City has made a dramatic turnaround. And in another small city, Rutland, Vermont, the Rutland Wal-Mart proves that even the nation's most famous superstore chain can participate in smart growth by converting an old, vacant, in-town property to a successful commercial venue.

On the smaller scale of mixed-use projects, the Denver Dry Goods building features shops, apartments, and condominiums in a single rehabilitated historic building. Second Street Studios in Santa Fe, New Mexico, also combines varied uses in one compact development, with an additional twist: some of the houses are split between work and living space, reducing residents' daily commuting distance to a flight of stairs.

Affordable Housing

To qualify as smart growth, the urban renaissance must not only work to the advantage of newcomers with high incomes, but also benefit current residents and those with lower incomes. Mixed-income housing allows urban revitalization without gentrification. Making mixed-income housing into a financially feasible reality can be challenging, but several of our examples show that it is being done successfully.

In two of our examples, low-income, minority communities took charge of their own development. With the Dudley Street Neighborhood Initiative in Boston, the city's poorest neighborhood created affordable housing through a community-controlled process, while also cleaning up its environment, attracting reinvestment, and improving social services. Pulaski Station in Chicago is another story about a low-income, minority community controlling its own redevelopment. Both communities successfully lobbied for the reopening of a neighborhood train station, recreating convenient connections to their cities' jobs and resources.

In other featured examples, municipalities work with specialized private developers to build mixed-income housing. Such a public/private partnership has brought historic renovation and sensitive, new residential development to Kansas City's Quality Hill. The neighborhood, close to downtown jobs and amenities, has again become very desirable, yet a substantial portion of the renovated and new units are reserved for lower-income families. Quality Hill's developer also created Westminster Place in St. Louis, Missouri, another public-private partnership, with half its housing in affordable units indistinguishable from those sold at market rates. A diverse set of families live in Westminster Place's verdant, suburban-style homes and shop in an adjacent shopping center, on a site that was previously one of the most troubled and crime-ridden neighborhoods in the city.

The Denver Dry Goods building, mentioned above, is yet another successful example of a smart-growth project with a diverse income mix—in this case, with affordable apartments in the same building as million-dollar luxury condominiums. And Southside Park Cohousing in Sacramento combines two unusual elements in one mixed-income residential community: it was planned by its own residents (not by a developer), and it places a strong emphasis on cooperation.

Recycling the Land, Reusing Old Buildings

Smart growth also stresses cleaning up and rebuilding abandoned parcels and buildings before building brand-new structures on virgin lands. Atlantic Station, mentioned above, provides a great example of this, since it is located on a cleaned-up industrial site. The Can Company, in Baltimore, is another brownfield (see Glossary) cleanup project that has transformed a century-old industrial site into a vibrant mix of high-tech offices, bookstore, shops, and restaurants. The Denver Dry Goods building, mentioned above for its mixed-use and mixed-income features, is another example of giving new life to an old building. The project took a landmark department store that had gone out of business and renovated it in an historically and environmentally sensitive way.

Hospitals present a special category among properties with opportunities for new uses. As changes in the medical service industry force more and more hospitals to close their doors, their often-large campuses are becoming available for redevelopment. Adidas Village in Portland provides a fine example of the creative use of old hospital property. It also illustrates corporate leadership in city revitalization and the business advantages of a smart-growth urban location.

Urban Renaissance and Smart Growth

Smart-growth advocates are keenly aware that every abandoned urban parcel or building that is redeveloped translates into farms, trees, or wetlands saved from being bulldozed for development somewhere else. Development will occur somewhere as long as the population is growing; instead of allowing growth to occur in a haphazard, inefficient fashion, we can encourage it to take place in or adjacent to existing communities. Cities, with their capacity for change, can accommodate well-planned growth without sacrificing livability. In doing so, they help save our countryside. Jane Jacobs was, once again, right: cities solve problems beyond their own boundaries.

ADIDAS VILLAGE
PORTLAND, OREGON

Employees of the athletic footwear and apparel giant Adidas were decidedly unhappy when the expanding AdidasUS headquarters was moved, in 1995, from Portland to one of its suburbs. The young, hip workforce disliked the sterility of their new surroundings, their long daily commutes, and their lack of

FROM A SUBURBAN CAMPUS TO AN URBAN VILLAGE

transportation choices. The suburban location also proved to have business disadvantages, because it was far from suppliers, the airport, and the smaller international branch of Adidas that remained in the city. As a result, after only a couple of years in the suburbs, Adidas's management decided to reverse course and seek a new site in the city. But where would the corporation find a sufficiently large, available site close to Portland's popular downtown? The answer was a property once occupied by a hospital.

The Hospital Property

Bess Kaiser Hospital was built in the early 1950s to provide health care to steel workers and their families from the Overlook and Mocks Crest areas of North Portland. Centrally located on a prominent bluff, the hospital was a community landmark and an important asset to nearby neighborhoods. When its parent corporation, Kaiser Permanente, decided in the 1990s to sell Bess Kaiser because of an oversupply of hospital beds in the area, among other reasons, it looked for a buyer that would be a good neighbor to the surrounding community. Kaiser even invited three neighborhood representatives to serve on its 12-person selection committee.

Twenty-five development companies expressed inter-

Adidas Village Plaza.

SOLVING SPRAWL

est in the property, but Jim Winkler, a Portland developer, submitted the winning plan. His proposal appealed to neighbors because it emphasized improving public spaces and amenities, along with using the existing buildings.

Winkler proposed to retrofit the Kaiser buildings for office use. He envisioned replacing the large surface parking lot with new buildings, public plazas, and an underground garage. Besides creating public gathering places, Winkler promised to develop public walking paths throughout the development, to improve pedestrian crossings on the busy avenue that bisects the property, and to provide such amenities as a community room, childcare center, or cafe. Winkler's ulti-

> **SMART-GROWTH FEATURES**
> ▶ Reuse of abandoned property
> ▶ Recycling of materials from old building
> ▶ New bus stops, bicycle path
> ▶ Neighborhood revitalization
> ▶ Inclusive, neighborhood-oriented planning process

mate hope was to find a progressive corporation that would locate its headquarters at the site. In Adidas, he found a perfect fit.

A Sports Village

Winkler and Adidas have spent the last few years generating extensive plans for what the new campus will look like. Adidas has embraced the developer's vision, adding its own identity as a sports-apparel manufacturer with European origins. The sports theme, in particular, will be expressed in practical as well as symbolic measures. The development's focal point will be an athletic facility, including a gymnasium and an adjacent soccer field, both of which will allow Adidas to test new products. The soccer field and part of the gym will be open to the public. The new buildings will be clustered around this athletic complex. Although they will be consistent with the architectural style of the old hospital, they will be accented with yellow, red, blue, and green touches, a reference to the colors of the Olympic rings.

> **PRINCIPALS**
> **Developer:** Winkler Corporation
> **Design:** BOORA Architects
> **Public sector:** Mayor's Office of Neighborhood Involvement, City of Portland
> **Other:** AdidasUS (single tenant); Overlook Neighborhood Association

Inspired by the Bavarian village where the company originated, the new headquarters will be called Adidas Village. In contrast to typical office campuses, such as rival Nike's gated headquarters in the Portland suburb of Beaverton, the village will not just be open to the public but will be inviting, with its pleasant and useful pedestrian network and public gathering places. Instead of isolating itself from the surrounding neighborhoods, the large complex actually provides better connections than those that existed when Bess Kaiser occupied the site. For example, to get to the Overlook neighborhood's main street, Greeley Avenue, residents must currently navigate a maze of paths and sidewalks. Once

SNAPSHOT: SMART GROWTH AND HOSPITAL CLOSINGS

The closing of Bess Kaiser Hospital in Portland is part of a nationwide trend. In recent decades, the economics of health care have changed, bringing sales, mergers, buyouts, managed care, and the conversion of hospitals to other health-care uses. An average of around 40 hospitals has closed each year in the past five years.

However, hospitals are often important landmarks and resources that have been in their communities for several generations. Neighborhood residents may develop sentimental ties to these institutions, where they or family members may have been born, sought treatment, or died. Hospitals not only represent convenient access to medical treatment for nearby residents but also provide security, job opportunity, social support, and community meeting places. A hospital closing can be particularly painful for a community.

What replaces the hospital becomes a crucial question. Usually, hospital property is large and offers many options for reuse, such as conversions to offices, educational institutions, or housing—even, in one instance, a sports complex. In almost every case, re-use is a beneficial smart-growth strategy.

AdidasUS's conversion of Bess Kaiser to its corporate headquarters, described in the adjoining text, is one such example. The conversion of Mercy Hospital in Detroit offers another good model. Established in 1923 by the Sisters of Mercy, the hospital grew into a large institution, counting 184,000 outpatient visits and operating 268 beds in the fiscal year ending in mid-1999. However, as a result of mounting losses, the hospital was forced to close at the end of that year.

Mercy's attractive 27-acre campus is located in a very depressed area on Detroit's east side. Mercy hired Dynamis Healthcare Advisors to interview neighbors about redevelopment options and found that they wanted a variety of social services, such as childcare, job training, and adult day care.

The solution was a multiuse facility. In August 2000, three groups announced joint ownership of Mercy: SER Metro, which runs citywide education, training, and employment programs for youths and adults; Boysville, which serves youths and their families in 30 locations in Michigan and Ohio; and Detroit YMCA. Trinity Health—Mercy's owner at the time of the closing—is retaining title to some of the property, in order to keep operating a primary-care clinic for the uninsured, and to open a 59-unit independent living facility for the elderly. The partners may also lease some of the property to other community organizations and the city.

Dynamis's president, Scott Keller, is pleased with the result. Hospitals "can close and take the heat," he told *Planning* magazine, or "go the extra year and really try to develop something that works." Both Mercy and Kaiser chose the second path, and the communities they leave behind are thankful for it.[1]

Adidas Village is built, a convenient pedestrian path will offer easy access. Adidas will also provide better bicycle lanes, a new traffic light, and a relocated bus stop on Greeley Avenue.

A Good Citizen and Neighbor

Bess Kaiser left behind many fixtures that were not needed in the new office, including doors, toilets, surgical equipment, and other building parts. Adidas decided to donate some 280 tons of the leftover equipment to developing countries, including Honduras and Kyrgystan.

The company also gave away shrubs and other landscaping that had to be uprooted because of renovation and construction. It donated funds for a children's playground and a basketball court in Madrona Park, a public park adjacent to the site on the south. Furthermore, Adidas will regrade Madrona's parking lot to create a better view and a more convenient link between the neighborhood and the park.

PROJECT DATA
- ▶ 13 acres
- ▶ 215,000 sq.ft. office space retrofitted from hospital use
- ▶ 137,000 sq.ft. new office space
- ▶ 18,000 sq.ft. athletic facility
- ▶ Underground garage

Adidas Village is expected to bring economic revitalization to the Overlook neighborhood. Although this part of North Portland is less than five miles from downtown, it has long been perceived as an industrial area. The planned arrival of a new light rail line—with a stop only four blocks from Adidas Village—and the very presence of the large corporate headquarters could fundamentally change that image. Already, new shops have opened in anticipation of a fresh clientele in the neighborhood. And the housing market might soon heat up as well, especially if many Adidas employees decide to live close to work.

Community members who were distraught when Bess Kaiser announced its departure now believe that Adidas will be a good corporate neighbor. Mary Lou Munroe, head of the Overlook Neighborhood Association, is enthusiastic about the Adidas headquarters. "It's going to be big. But it's going to improve our community."

ATLANTIC STATION
ATLANTA, GEORGIA

Scattered over an area larger than the state of Delaware, the Atlanta region's workers face the nation's longest average commute and some of its most congested freeways. Ozone smog levels are so bad that, in 1998, a federal judge ordered a moratorium on road projects requiring federal approval until local

BROWNFIELD REDEVELOPMENT HELPS CLEAN THE AIR

agencies could come up with a better plan to improve regional air quality. Indeed, the region suffered 69 ozone alert days in 1999. (The legal status of the region's air-quality deficiencies remains in litigation as this book goes to publication.)

Ironically, this ban could have stopped a project with the potential to enhance air quality: the redevelopment of an urban brownfield into a transit-accessible and pedestrian-friendly complex of offices, homes, and shops. Situated close to midtown Atlanta, the development would attract residents and businesses back to the city. But the location in question, a former steel mill, was cut off from midtown, requiring that a new bridge be built to connect the development to the rest of the city. Unfortunately, the bridge fell under the road-building moratorium. The developers overcame the hurdle with the help of the U.S. Environmental Protection Agency (EPA), which found the development's potential air-quality benefits so compelling that the bridge qualified for an exemption from the court's order.

A rendering of Atlantic Station.

The new development, Atlantic Station (also sometimes called Atlantic Steel, after the abandoned facility on its site), is now under construction. It points the way to a more sustainable future in the Atlanta region and provides a national model for improving the environment through smart growth.

ATLANTIC STATION, LLC

An Ambitious and Diverse Plan

In 1997, Jacoby Development, Inc., bought the Atlantic Station site. The developer envisioned a "city within the city"—a connected community with offices, houses, and shops linked by bicycle lanes, walking paths, streets, and public transportation.

Such a project was far from business as usual in metropolitan Atlanta, where in recent years each one percent growth in population has corresponded with an increase of 10 to 20 percent in developed land. The resulting sprawl has made most of the region's residents completely dependent on their cars and forced them into long commutes. But Atlantic Station, with its central location, good transit access, and mix of residences, offices, and entertainment venues within walking distance, promised many benefits that would be accessible without using a car.

> **SMART-GROWTH FEATURES**
> ▶ Brownfield cleanup
> ▶ Compact, infill development
> ▶ Mix of housing, offices, entertainment, hotels, and more
> ▶ Easy access to subway station and other transit options
> ▶ Community involvement in planning process
> ▶ Quantified air-quality benefits over comparable sprawl developments

EPA Studies Predict Air Quality Benefits

But first, there was the issue of the bridge. Atlantic Station is bounded to the north by railroad tracks and to the east by two interstate highways, cutting it off from midtown Atlanta. Without the bridge connecting it to midtown, redeveloping the site would not be feasible.

The developer applied for special approval under an EPA pilot program called Project XL. EPA had established Project XL two years earlier to give businesses and communities more freedom to develop innovative strategies to comply with environmental laws, so long as it is clear that the strategies will increase environmental benefits beyond those expected from a conventional approach. Although the results of Project XL across the country have so far been mixed for the environment, this time it produced a winner.

To determine Atlantic Station's potential benefits, EPA used a complex modeling process. It chose three metropolitan Atlanta sites big enough to absorb projects of Atlantic Station's size and then modeled the transportation and emissions impacts of hypothetical projects at each one, comparing them to projections for Atlantic Station. Two of the models were standard low-density suburban developments—those most typical for the region. The third was more in keeping with a smart-growth philosophy: it had relatively high density, an urban-style street pattern, and rail transit, but was located in an Atlanta suburb.

All three sites were projected to generate more driving and worse air emissions than Atlantic Station. In particular, Atlantic Station was shown to be likely to produce only half as much driving as the two low-density projects, and 14 percent less than the compact suburban development. And the reduced driving associated with Atlantic Station promised dramatic benefits for air quality: nitrogen oxide emissions would be 81, 72.5 and 37 percent higher at the three suburban sites than at Atlantic Station. Emissions of volatile organic compounds, the other major precursor to ozone smog, were also projected to be substantially higher at the other sites.

EPA also identified other environmental benefits of Atlantic Station, such as dramatically lower emissions of carbon dioxide, the principal gas that causes global warming. The benefits also included the brownfield remediation, conservation of open space, improved neighborhood amenities, and new housing opportunities. Stan Meiburg, EPA's deputy administrator, explained the significance of these findings to the *Atlanta Journal-Constitution*: "If you're going to see growth in an area like Atlanta, the growth from infill produces less air quality impact than sprawling into a new area."[2]

As a result of its findings, the EPA designated Atlantic Station's redevelopment a "transportation control measure," a classification for actions that improve air quality through more efficient transportation patterns. The designation exempted the bridge from the moratorium, allowing the project to move forward.

Making a Good Project Even Better

Seeing Atlantic Station as a potential national model, the EPA also contributed resources to further improving its design. The agency commissioned the innovative Miami architectural firm Duany Plater-Zyberk & Company (DPZ) to conduct a design charette (see Glossary), or brainstorming session, with stakeholders, and to recommend improvements. The charette allowed community members, government

1997: Jacoby Development purchases Atlantic Station site   **October 1998:** EPA accepts Project XL proposal   **September 1999:** Atlantic Station Project XL agreement signed   **Fall 1999:** Demolition and remediation begin   **Fall 2000:** New construction begins   **Fall 2002:** Expected Phase 1 opening (residential, retail, office, hotel)   **Fall 2006:** Expected Phase 2 completion

agencies, prospective developers, and other interested parties to voice their concerns about and hopes for the site. DPZ incorporated these comments and recommended better connections to nearby streets, traffic-calming measures, clearer walking routes, a more thorough mix of uses, and a more efficient layout. The developer adopted many of the DPZ recommendations.

Indeed, Jacoby Development has sought community input in all stages of its planning for Atlantic Station. For example, in a 1999 workshop, residents of the Home Park neighborhood, which is adjacent to the site, requested new green spaces and an extension of existing Home Park streets into Atlantic Station, which Jacoby has promised to provide. The company has also worked to create design elements that will meld the two neighborhoods.

> **PRINCIPALS**
> **Developer:** Jacoby Development; Post Properties; The Mills Corporation
> **Design:** Thompson, Ventullet, & Stainback; Duany Plater-Zyberk & Company
> **Public sector:** U.S. Environmental Protection Agency; City of Atlanta
> **Other:** Home Park Community Improvement Association

Today, the plan calls for a 138-acre, 12-million-square-foot development, including parks, lakes, and other urban refuges. It will also contain 3,200 residential units, a high-technology center with four to five million square feet of office space, four hotels with 1,000 rooms, and 1.5 million square feet of space for shopping and entertainment.

Cleanup and Construction

In the fall of 1999, developers began the cleanup of the site, where heavy metals had been milled for a century. It is the largest cleanup of an industrial site ever to take place in the southeastern United States. Some of the soil will be shipped to special landfills, and some will be encapsulated on the site in cement foundations, parking decks, or other areas. The site will also be required to monitor its soil and groundwater.

And what about the bridge? It is slated for construction from 2001 to 2003. The 130-foot-wide structure will span Interstate Highways 75 and 85, and include wide sidewalks, bicycle and transit lanes, benches, trees, and four general traffic lanes, as well as a separate pathway for a future rail connection to MARTA, Atlanta's rapid transit system.

The bridge to Atlantic Station is a symbolic bridge to Atlanta's future. Atlantic Station shows that smarter growth is possible, even in Atlanta. And the EPA studies (which will continue to monitor the site's transportation and air impact performance for ten years) show that we can also confidently anticipate significant environmental benefits from this new approach to development. In the words of Atlanta Mayor Bill Campbell, "This is the most important development project in Atlanta in the last 50 years, bar none."

SNAPSHOT: **SMART GROWTH AND AIR QUALITY**

Sprawl development causes increased automobile dependence and longer driving distances, which in turn result in significant emissions of air pollutants. Despite improvements in clean vehicle technology, today's average passenger car continues to emit 557 pounds of carbon monoxide, 75 pounds of volatile organic compounds, a precursor to ozone smog, and 39 pounds of nitrogen oxides, another smog precursor, each year. A typical auto-dependent suburban shopping center has been found to cause the emission of over half the nitrogen oxides of a major power plant, five times the organic gases, and over 30 times the carbon monoxide, all because of related vehicle travel.

Pollutants from motor vehicles are associated with asthma and a range of other serious and even fatal health problems. Although the number varies from year to year because of variations in the weather—hot days stimulate the formation of smog if the requisite chemical ingredients are present—around 90 metro areas in the U.S. regularly violated federal smog standards in the 1990s. In addition, motor vehicles, particularly diesel-powered buses and freight trucks, constitute a significant source of soot and other airborne fine particles that, when inhaled, lodge in and damage human tissue.

Smart growth reduces vehicle emissions by reducing automobile dependence and shortening driving distances. Portland, Oregon, which has made substantial investments in public transit, walkable neighborhoods around transit stops, and preservation of open space around its metro area, reduced by 86 percent the number of days its air quality violated federal smog standards from the mid-1980s to the mid-1990s; in the same period, sprawling Atlanta, Georgia, with comparable rates of population and job growth but no smart-growth measures, suffered an increase in smoggy days. At the neighborhood level, EPA research on Atlantic Station (see adjacent text) shows a dramatic reduction in air pollutant emissions as compared to sprawling developments. This is consistent with a large body of research demonstrating reduced rates of driving in walkable neighborhoods, particularly those with good transit service and a mix of uses.[3]

THE CAN COMPANY
BALTIMORE, MARYLAND

Like many other factories built in the heyday of the Industrial Revolution, the American Can Company's complex became obsolete by the end of the twentieth century. As a result of a merger in the late 1980s, the facility was closed and 800 employees were let go. Its dozen buildings dating from the late 1800s and early 1900s remained vacant and decaying. What would become of this relic of the industrial past?

**FROM
TIN CANS
TO HIGH-TECH**

Recycling the Can

In 1987, Baltimore received a federal urban development assistance grant, $8.5 million of which was directed towards clearing and redeveloping the American Can site. But the city's original redevelopment concept, which called for razing all but one building and erecting two high-rise residential towers, met with strong opposition from residents of the Canton community where the complex was located. A generation had grown up when the can factory was a major presence in the neighborhood, and they wanted to save the historically significant buildings. They started a campaign, Recycle The Can, to promote a more preservation-oriented redevelopment.

The city eventually abandoned its plan, the grant was spent elsewhere, and the can manufacturing buildings were left standing but vacant. The neighbors who formed the Recycle The Can campaign would have to wait ten years before a proposal they liked came along. But, during this time, important changes were taking place in the community.

In the 1990s, Canton started to rebound. The success of Baltimore's famous Inner Harbor was spilling over to the city's other waterfront neighborhoods, connected by a convenient water taxi system and by a pedestrian and bike path. In Canton, land along the waterfront that had been cleared for an abandoned highway project now

SMART-GROWTH FEATURES
- ▶ Renovation and reuse of an abandoned factory
- ▶ Diverse mix of offices, shops, and restaurants
- ▶ Brownfield cleanup
- ▶ Neighborhood involvement
- ▶ Neighborhood revitalization and new jobs

The Can Company before.

attracted investors, who built condominiums for middle- to higher-income residents. Further inland, young urban professionals, lured by Canton's afford-ability and convenience to downtown, began renovating row houses. Restaurants and bars opened. And in 1994, the eastern half of the American Can property was sold to the Safeway super-market chain, which demol-ished all its buildings (they happened to be the historically less significant ones) to build a 50,000-square-foot store and parking lot.

Salvaging, Repairing, and Restoring

A more ambitious plan for the remaining 4.3 acres began to emerge from a local developer and builder, Bill Struever of Struever Bros. Eccles & Rouse (SBE&R), a firm well known for several other pro-jects reusing old industrial structures in Baltimore, including some other canneries. This time with the community's support, SBE&R renovated the complex's five most historic and characteristic buildings and filled them with a diverse mix of offices, shops, and restaurants.

It was not an easy or simple process. By 1997, when SBE&R ac-quired the site, the abandoned cannery's brick and concrete buildings were in abysmal condition. Windows were bent, broken, or filled in; walls were scarred and covered with years of paint and graffiti; roofs were leaking. SBE&R had to restore the windows, reglaze 15,000 panes of glass, repair and repoint the brick walls, construct new roofs, salvage and restore the distinctive stacks, ventilators, and monitors on the roofs—all in less than a year, when the first tenant was slated to arrive.

To complicate matters further, a portion of the site's soil had been contaminated with lead. SBE&R became the first company to take advantage of the Brownfields Voluntary Cleanup Program administered by the state of Maryland, which gives new owners of con-

PRINCIPALS

Developer: Struever Bros. Eccles & Rouse, Inc.
Design: Design Collective, Inc
Public sector: State of Maryland
Other: NASA (investor in ETC building)

SOLVING SPRAWL

taminated sites limited lia-
bility relief for past contamination in exchange for
meeting cleanup require-
ments. A goldfish pond,
beautified by water lilies
and ornamental grasses,
now sits on the formerly
lead-contaminated site.

A Mix of Tenants

The Can Company hosts an
impressive array of tenants.
One of the most unusual is

The Can Company
after.

a high-tech incubator called the Emerging Technology Center (ETC).
The center can accommodate up to 30 start-up technology companies, offering them subsidized rent, shared administrative resources,
and access to the state's academic institutions and to NASA's technology outreach program. Since the incubator had the potential to boost
desired local economic activity, a number of entities decided to support it. In particular, the ETC was funded by $1 million from the
state, $800,000 from NASA, $1 million from other federal sources,
$500,000 from Baltimore, and $600,000 from SBE&R. Today, the
ETC enjoys high demand and is already fully leased.

Independent of the ETC, another new, technology-oriented company called Gr8 decided to set up shop at the Can Company. Its work
encompasses graphic design, marketing, computer programming, and
web page design. This mix has proven very successful; in just a few
years, the company grew from two to 64 employees. The firm's cutting-
edge mentality is reflected in the interior design of the Gr8 office.
They chose to celebrate, rather than hide, the building interior's
industrial past, leaving most of the building systems exposed. Using
such prosaic building materials as plywood, corrugated metal, and fiber-
glass sheets, they created a workspace that feels both futuristic and historic at the same time.

A more traditional manufacturer also found the Can Company
highly desirable. DAP Products, the world's largest manufacturer of
sealants and adhesives, relocated its 40,000-square-foot world headquarters to the site from a rural setting in Ohio, where few amenities
were within walking distance. This move brought about 100 jobs to

Baltimore. The first tenant to sign on, DAP had first choice of space in the facility. It chose to locate in the distinctive red-brick Norton Tin Can building, which was renovated—as were all buildings on the site—using DAP's own caulk, adhesives, and preservatives. Like others, DAP had fun designing a unique office space, which features corrugated metal walls, steel beams, wooden columns, a diner-style counter instead of a lunch table, and a grand staircase leading from one level of open, light-filled work space to another. "We could have gone to . . . a building with four walls and no character," says John McLaughlin, DAP's president and chief executive officer. "But this space has enormous energy. It's more fun. It's more conducive to communication. People are genuinely excited to come to work."

The shops and restaurants at the Can Company provide a multitude of amenities for office workers and neighborhood residents. Some even serve as regional attractions. Bibelot, for example, is a large independent bookstore that also features music. The Can Company store is Bibelot's third in the area, but the first in an urban location. Next to Bibelot is the popular Donna's Cafe. For those with larger appetites, there is the Austin Grill serving Tex-Mex food in an upbeat environment, or a more subdued seafood restaurant, the Atlantic. Good aromas also waft out of the Hudson Street Bakery. A variety of smaller shops, offering goods ranging from bridal wear to wine, rounds out the mix.

It is clear that the neighborhood, the city, and the businesses that moved into the Can Company have all benefited from the adaptive

SNAPSHOT: MARYLAND'S SMART-GROWTH PROGRAM

The Can Company was renovated with the support of Maryland's innovative and multi-faceted smart-growth program, which comprises a variety of inducements for nonsprawling development, including the brownfields measure discussed in the adjacent narrative. SBE&R also qualified for the program's Heritage Preservation Income Tax Credit, for rehabilitating a certified, historically significant structure. And, since the Can Company is located in a state priority funding area where growth has been determined by the affected community to be desirable, the state provided investments for infrastructure and economic development. For example, qualifying tenants received Job Creation Income Tax Credits, and state financial assistance created an incubator to assist new companies in the high-technology sector.

reuse (see Glossary) of the old can manufacturing plant. The project has also proved to be an economic success, with both SBE&R and its equity partner, the American Communities Fund of Fannie Mae (the federally chartered mortgage institution), receiving a good return on their high-risk investments.

Bill Struever once described the Can Company as "a wonderful project waiting to happen." With thousands of interesting industrial buildings still sitting vacant in many cities, many more of these projects are still ready and waiting.

DALLAS UPTOWN
DALLAS, TEXAS

Where in the United States are the great city neighborhoods? Cities on the East and West Coasts, such as San Francisco, New York, or Boston come to mind. Few would think of Sunbelt cities, which are better known for their explosive suburban growth and car-dependent lifestyles. But in Dallas, a reborn neighborhood is defying those stereotypes.

CITY DISTRICT OFFERS FREEDOM FROM THE CAR

Paradise for City Lovers

Dallas Uptown is a city lover's paradise. Located just north of downtown Dallas, its apartments, townhouses, and lofts are only a short walk from restaurants, pubs, cafes, gyms, galleries, museums, and nightclubs, as well as a large concentration of jobs within a three-mile radius. The *Dallas Morning News* painted a compelling picture of Uptown's urban features:

> Parts of Uptown . . . are beautifully set up for street life. Sidewalks are broad, often bricked. Trees shade them. Benches line them. Streetlights cast a soft glow on them. Cars park on streets without meters. Balconies open to the sidewalks. At night, rooftop gardens feature a glittering backdrop of skyline. Courtyards with flowers and statues are glimpsed through doorways. The soft splash of fountains can be heard. . . . People who live here walk to work. They wave at neighbors passing on the sidewalk. They go to museums and plays. They deal with shopkeepers who will run a tab without a credit card.[4]

Less than two decades ago, the area could be more accurately described as an urban nightmare. The neighborhood suffered from disinvestment, crime, and decrepit infrastructure—urban ills that have plagued many inner-city neighborhoods around the country. What was once one of Dallas's most affluent areas had become one of its most undesirable. Nevertheless, speculators bought and cleared land in the 1980s in the area,

SMART-GROWTH FEATURES
- ▶ City neighborhood in the midst of an automobile-oriented metropolis
- ▶ Revitalization of a run-down area
- ▶ Diverse mix of homes, offices, restaurants, galleries, shops
- ▶ Streets designed for walking as well as driving
- ▶ Public/private cooperation

hoping for a new wave of office development. Their hopes turned sour when the real estate market collapsed in the mid-1980s.

PRINCIPALS
Developer: Post Properties, Inc (formerly Columbus Realty, Inc)
Design: RTKL Associates
Public sector: City of Dallas

But the weak market created favorable conditions for building new housing in Uptown. When land prices are high, developers usually prefer to build office space, because of its much greater return on their high upfront investments. Low land prices in Dallas made housing development economically feasible close to the central business district.

Seizing the opportunity, Columbus Realty Trust (now Post Properties) bought eight properties in the Uptown area, with plans to build apartments, lofts, and townhouses within walking distance of the area's existing businesses on McKinney Avenue. In 1988, Columbus formed a partnership with the city of Dallas to revitalize the area. The city created a tax increment-financing (TIF) district, which allowed a portion of tax revenues collected in the area to be dedicated to improving the district's infrastructure. The water and sewage systems were revamped, utilities were buried, and streets were repaved.

A Developer's Dedication Turns "Folly" into Success

With improved infrastructure in place, the developers began sketching out their plans for the residences. Art Lomenick of Columbus/Post described the development company's approach: "When we first decided to move into Uptown, we became passionate about urban housing. It became a strong personal interest and much more than a business strategy. The studies went beyond books: I was constantly looking at urban form details: stoops, storefronts, doorknobs, cornices, court yards, and pocket parks."

Columbus launched its Uptown building boom in 1991 with the Meridian at State-Thomas, a 132-unit luxury apartment complex derided as folly by Dallas's real estate community. However, the pioneer effort proved that there was pent-up demand for high-quality city living in the Dallas

Bell tower in Dallas Uptown Village.

© STEVE HINDS PHOTOGRAPHY

market. Within weeks, every unit in the Meridian was leased. Uptown's next three residential complexes were equally successful.

In 1993, the Dallas City Council approved the creation of the Uptown Public Improvement District, in which property owners pay a special assessment to cover varied improvements throughout the district. (Such arrangements, usually called business improvement districts or BIDs, are becoming increasingly popular. See the box in our discussion of the MCI Center for an example in Washington, D.C.) Funds have been devoted primarily to security, special events, and capital improvements, including sidewalks, street lighting, and small public parks. Also in 1993, Columbus merged with Post Properties, another company dedicated to urban revitalization through developing high-quality rental properties.

Other developers took notice of the changes in Uptown, resulting in a wave of investment. Businesses flourished as more and more people moved to the neighborhood. By 1998, there were 56 restaurants in the 128-block area. The neighborhood also has a large grocery and drug store, a hardware store, several gyms, and a number of smaller specialty shops.

The Uptown World

An important aspect of Uptown's appeal is that many of its attractions are within walking distance. Wide tree-shaded brick sidewalks connect residential areas with work places, quiet neighborhood parks, and the hopping bars, cafes, and entertainment venues on McKinney Avenue. The city's only trolley line also runs along McKinney, providing another attractive alternative to driving. It is not uncommon to find Uptown residents like Sandra Christie, who estimates that she had put only 6,000 miles on her car in the six years she had lived in the neighborhood.[5]

Uptown is providing the urban character that its name promises. The housing stock is varied, including both new and renovated buildings, and comprising lofts, luxury units, and townhouses, all at a range of prices. But the new neighborhood is also predominantly affluent: the average Uptown household income was $99,000 per year in 1998, suggesting that, unfortunately, not all people can enjoy its urban delights.

For those who can, Uptown offers convenience, community, and freedom from their cars. As Ron Baker, a businessman, explains: "I could have gotten a large place for less money in North Dallas or Addison, but I didn't want the suburban feel. And there's just a lot of very positive energy here."[6] As Uptown proves, there is a very real market for urban living.

DENVER DRY GOODS

DENVER, COLORADO

T he late 1980s found Denver's downtown in the middle of a major recession and urban exodus. By some accounts, it was the worst time since the Great Depression. The savings and loan crisis hit Denver especially hard; at the same time, petroleum companies—an important component of the local econ-

REBIRTH OF 100-YEAR-OLD DOWNTOWN BUILDING

omy—were cutting staff or leaving Denver altogether. Downtown vacancy rates soared, hitting a high of 30.5 percent in 1988. Department stores and businesses were closing. The vacated Central Bank Building, once a great historic structure, was demolished for a parking lot because renovation would have been too expensive.

A Historic Department Store Barely Escapes the Wrecking Ball

Locals wondered if the city's hundred-year-old premier department store would share a similar fate. The Denver Dry Goods building, originally named McNamara Dry Goods, was built in 1888 and expanded three times through 1924. Generations of Denver residents shopped in the fashionable downtown store, or dined and socialized in its regal 800-seat Tea Room. But that era came to an end in 1987, when May Department Stores purchased the Denver Dry Goods chain and closed the store to prevent competition with its own

downtown location. After a year of failed attempts to sell the building, May was about to give up on the 350,000-square-foot vacant structure.

Fortunately, the city's redevelopment agency, the Denver Urban Renewal Authority (DURA), stepped in and purchased the building for $7.5 million. DURA hoped that redevelopment of the centrally-located

Relaxation and shopping at Denver Dry Goods.

landmark would not only protect a historic structure, but also help revitalize the surrounding area.

But it would take years to even find a fiscally viable development proposal. Between 1988 and 1992, DURA joined with a succession of four private developers, only to see each plan fail. None of the developers could attract sufficient financing. Major lenders considered downtown Denver undesirable and unprofitable; in fact, there was a virtual halt to real estate loans in Denver at this time, and it was equally difficult to lure tenants downtown. The Denver Dry Goods building's future remained uncertain.

A Successful Partnership, at Last

DURA's perseverance, help from the mayor, and the talent of a visionary developer began to turn the tide in 1992. In particular, Mayor Wellington Webb, who was committed to redeveloping downtown, helped convince the Metro Convention and Visitors' Bureau to lease 20,000 square feet of office space on the building's third floor at market-rate rent. DURA then formed a successful partnership with a private developer, Jonathan Rose of the New York-based Affordable Housing Development Corporation (AHDC), who brought expertise, commitment, and a new vision to the project. "I choose projects that can become models for change," Rose explained. "The Denver Dry had that potential. Developing mixed-income projects is not easy, so I also look for buildings, like this one, that I can love."

Rose helped secure such innovative new financing sources as historic-building tax credits, low-income-housing tax credits, and tax increment financing, which allows some tax revenues to be allocated toward infrastructure improvements. In the end, 23 financing sources had to be pulled together to make the project a reality.

The key to the new development plan's success was splitting the building into distinct parts. Financing was easier to secure for these smaller, separate units. The different uses added up to a vibrant mix—shops, offices, affordable and market-rate apartments, and luxury condominiums—all in one building.

In the spring of 1993, longtime Denverites were astonished as they watched the familiar white paint of the former department store disappear and a red-brick and sandstone beauty emerge

Live/work studio in the Denver Dry Goods Building.

under the scaffolding. To restore the original look of the building, 30 coats of paint had to be laboriously removed.

But while the outside of the building regained its former red brick, its contents took on an entirely new look. The first tenant was a well-known local camera store. Today, the old department store is also home to retailers of computer software, video games, and CDs. These shops, along with clothier T.J. Maxx, take up the basement, the ground floor and part of the second floor. The Visitors Bureau and DURA are on the second and third floors.

The fourth through sixth floors feature a diverse mix of residential units. Fifty-one are rental apartments. Thirty-nine of them are priced to be affordable, for people earning 60 percent or less of the median income. Office clerks, service sector employees, and others who work in downtown's lower-paying jobs find these apartments very attractive. They are both within walking distance or a convenient transit ride to work, and within their budgets.

The rental apartments, shops, and offices were completed by the partnership between DURA and Rose in 1994. The remaining parts of the upper floors were sold to another developer, BCORP Holdings, for condominium development. In May 2000, the company sold the last of its 66 lofts: the Tea Room. With its 4,500 interior square feet, huge wraparound deck, vaulted ceilings, and painted frescoes, the Tea Room is an opulent space, with a price to match. It sold for nearly $1.35 million. Its owners share the building with residents of apartments renting for less than $600 per month—a testament to Denver Dry Goods's success in attracting mixed incomes as well as mixed uses.

A Green Building

The Denver Dry Building of today is a green development for many reasons. The very fact that the two-block, seven-level building was saved and remodeled means significant energy savings over new construction of similar size. Moreover, a number of innovative energy

SNAPSHOT: DOWNTOWN HOUSING IN DENVER

Downtowns need residents to thrive. A catalyst for turning around Denver's deeply troubled central district was the conversion of old warehouses into sought-after loft apartments in Lower Downtown (LoDo). In the late 1980s, in the midst of Denver's recession, the city council approved historic-district designation for a 20-block area of turn-of-the-century warehouses and industrial buildings in LoDo. Without this designation, many of the buildings might have been demolished; in fact, about 20 percent of the buildings had already been razed in just the previous seven years, often to build parking lots. The new historic district's zoning was also revised to support redevelopment of older buildings, and a bond issue provided funds for sprucing up the streets.

In spite of these incentives, it took a pioneering developer's success to start the wave of loft conversions. Dana Crawford, known in the Denver community for her commercial historic preservation projects, began her first LoDo residential project in 1990 by renovating an 1890s-era warehouse. By the time all the warehouse's units were completed, more than half were already sold, revealing the strong pent-up demand for downtown loft living. Crawford's second warehouse conversion was equally successful, convincing other developers to follow suit.

Between 1990 and 1997, more than 450 LoDo lofts were built. Restaurants, cafes, nightclubs, and shops followed in their wake, transforming the once run-down neighborhood of vacant industrial buildings into a lively, desirable urban neighborhood.

The wave of residential development has now reached other parts of downtown and the surrounding neighborhoods, broadening the range of housing choices in the city. Unlike in trendy LoDo, where lofts are now commanding top prices, affordable rental and for-sale units are available in these other up-and-coming neighborhoods. For example, in the central business district, five old bank and office buildings were converted to a mixture of 430 low-income and market-rate rental units. And, in Denver's diverse Uptown, a 10.5-acre vacant hospital campus is being redeveloped as a mixture of ground-floor businesses, restaurants, small offices, and 1,100 residential units. What started with LoDo is now a full-blown renaissance of in-city living.

features were included in the redevelopment, including insulated-glass windows (made to fit the old historic frames), and sophisticated heating and cooling systems that make extensive use of natural systems. The renovated building uses 60 percent less energy than the old department store.

In addition, the availability of a variety of transportation options is among the Denver Dry's most environmentally significant features. The downtown location is accessible by foot, bicycle, and public transit. It is located at the intersection of the city's light-rail system and 16th Street Mall shuttle, and near many bus stops. Rose estimates that the residential apartments average less than one vehicle apiece, and most residents who do have cars use them sparingly. To satisfy retailers that there would be sufficient customer parking, Rose went to great lengths to identify parking options and set up a voucher system—but the retailers didn't need it.

A Model for Mixed-Use Historic Development Downtown

By the late 1990s, downtown Denver was on the rebound. Many factors contributed, including better economic times, an aggressive capital improvement program, and the birth of a new residential and entertainment district in Lower Downtown (see adjacent discussion). But the early success of the Denver Dry Goods redevelopment was an important catalyst for change. It sparked development interest in mixed-use historic projects, and provided a template for structuring and financing them. More than 20 similar mixed-use projects have been developed downtown, bringing people, money, and excitement back into the heart of Denver.

The Denver Dry Goods Building also serves as a symbol for the comeback of the city. As architect Jennifer Moulton, director of Denver's Planning and Community Development Office, put it: "This building used to be a symbol of our terrible economy. But now it's a symbol of our rebirth."[7]

DUDLEY STREET NEIGHBORHOOD INITIATIVE
BOSTON, MASSACHUSETTS

The characteristics that make a city neighborhood great are by no means restricted to upscale developments. Indeed, sometimes older, low- or moderate-income neighborhoods exhibit greater continuity and stronger bonds—a stronger sense of what we call "community"—than do those with higher incomes. As a result, they can sometimes be the source of extraordinary achievements in urban revitalization. There may be no more inspiring example of this than the neighborhood surrounding Boston's Dudley Street, an avenue that runs through the city's Roxbury district.

A STRUGGLING BOSTON NEIGHBORHOOD TAKES CHARGE OF ITS FUTURE

Down, but Not Out

Less than two miles from downtown Boston, the Dudley Street neighborhood is one of the poorest in Massachusetts, with per capita income half that of Boston as a whole, and unemployment at least twice as high. Yet Jay Walljasper, a reporter with *The Nation* who visited the area, observed in 1997 that "you also see giggling kids walking home from school, old ladies tending flower patches in their side yards and neighbors chatting over fences behind tidy white wood-frame houses . . . you still sense something of the idealized America found on Normal Rockwell's *Saturday Evening Post* covers."[8]

There is a reason why Walljasper found Dudley Street to be strong and hopeful despite lingering poverty. The secret is a fifteen-year-old community-driven revitalization effort called the Dudley Street Neighborhood Initiative.

The initiative was sorely needed. For years, the area around Dudley Street suffered from

Dudley Street's children on the job.

DUDLEY STREET NEIGHBORHOOD INITIATIVE

disinvestment, redlining, arson, and illegal dumping. Between 1947 and 1976, half the neighborhood's housing stock was demolished or destroyed by fire. By the 1980s, more than a third of its land was vacant. The abandoned lots were filled with wrecked cars, weeds, and

trash. Businesses fled; drug dealers took over run-down playgrounds. The neighborhood became the poorest in Boston, overlooked by city services and becoming, in effect, a dumping ground for the rest of the city.

Yet the human capital was diverse and strong. Once an Irish and Italian neighborhood, the Dudley Street area had become a melting pot: 40 percent African American, 29 percent Latino, 25 percent Cape Verdean (from islands off the west coast of Africa), and 7 percent white.[9] These groups came together to create a vibrant, multicultural vision for their neighborhood.

The Community Takes Charge

In the early 1980s, a social service agency approached the Riley Foundation, a local philanthropic organization, with its concerns about the area, and the foundation decided in 1984 to make a substantial investment in revitalizing Roxbury and North Dorchester, an adjoining neighborhood. But the foundation's good intentions were quickly met with suspicion from neighborhood residents, who were distrustful because they had been allotted only three seats on the 23-member board proposed to oversee the effort.

In response, a group of residents convinced the foundation to underwrite a revitalization process that would be led by the neighborhood itself rather than by outsiders. The result was the Dudley Street Neighborhood Initiative (DSNI), created in 1985 with a strong grassroots focus. The initiative's membership and its board consist mostly of neighborhood residents, along with local social service agencies, small businesses, and religious institutions. The residents on the board come from all of the neighborhood's ethnic groups. There is also a youth representative.

In 1986, DSNI coordinated a neighborhood "visioning" process, in which stakeholders were invited to imagine the community's future.

With the help of expert consultants, the initiative sponsored a series of focus groups, committee and community meetings, and brain-storming sessions. More than 200 residents participated in the eight-month process. The result was the DSNI Revitalization Plan, completed and adopted by the city in 1987. (It was updated in 1996.)

PRINCIPALS

Public sector: City of Boston
Grassroots: Dudley Street Neighborhood Initiative; Dudley Neighbors, Incorporated
Other: Riley Foundation; Ford Foundation

The plan, still in effect, is notable for its comprehension and bold optimism about the neighborhood's potential. It emphasizes building community spirit as much as erecting new homes. It provides for development of substantial new housing, along with bike paths, apple orchards, outdoor cafes, community gardens, fountains, art programs, and a town common for concerts. It also seeks to meet pressing economic needs like jobs. The goal is to create and maintain a vibrant "urban village."

"Don't Dump on Us"

While dreams have always been integral to the initiative's vision, its organizing campaigns in the late 1980s and early 1990s first had to address some pressing real-life problems. DSNI's initial organized campaign tackled a particularly serious nuisance undermining the quality of life in the Dudley Street neighborhood: illegal dumping. Dozens of wrecked cars were abandoned on the neighborhood's streets each week, and illegal junkyards and trash transfer stations operated on vacant lots and in back alleys in the light of day. "You had to hold your nose when you drove down the road," Che Madyun, a former DSNI board president, told *The Nation*. "It was terrible."[10]

Organizing under the slogan "Don't Dump on Us," neighborhood residents erected signs, closed off lots that served as dumping grounds, and successfully lobbied city hall to take action. Mayor Ray Flynn put his weight behind the cleanup effort. Gradually, the situation improved.

But years of neglect had left a lingering impact. Over 50 hazardous waste sites have been identified within and around the borders of the 1.5-square-mile Dudley neighborhood. Most of these sites were contaminated with petroleum from underground storage tanks. Since 1994, DSNI has led community involvement in remediation efforts led by environmental authorities. In a related environmental initiative, DSNI has also undertaken a campaign to reduce exposure to lead, through methods ranging from community education to testing soil.

Building the Village

To oversee the housing development in the neighborhood, DSNI created an urban community land trust, Dudley Neighbors, Incorporated. The trust acquires land and issues leases to developers and subsequently to individual homeowners, cooperative housing corporations, and other forms of limited partnerships. By using 99-year leases, Dudley Neighbors can provide stability to its lessees while assuring that its properties are used for purposes compatible with the community's vision. It can also establish guidelines for the sale and resale prices of homes.

An abundance of abandoned lots belonging to absentee owners posed a challenging roadblock to the trust's work. In the 60-acre Dudley Triangle area, the most distressed part of the Dudley Street neighborhood, more than one-fifth of the land was vacant. Some 130 private owners held half of this vacant land, while the city had acquired the other half, mostly as a result of tax delinquencies. Dudley Neighbors convinced the city to deed its share to the neighborhood. But acquiring the other half from land speculators and unwilling sellers promised to be difficult and prohibitively expensive.

The trust got around this problem by applying to the city's redevelopment agency for recognition as an "urban redevelopment corporation" under Massachusetts law. This would allow Dudley Neighbors

Some of Dudley's housing and green space.

to use a tool that had not before been granted to a neighborhood organization: the power of eminent domain to acquire private property even from unwilling owners for the public good in return for just compensation. Showing extraordinary confidence in the work of DSNI and its land trust, the agency approved the request in 1988. There were legal challenges, but the trust's right to administer eminent domain in the Triangle was upheld after four years of litigation.

Even though land values in the Triangle had long been depressed, acquiring a critical mass of land for redevelopment was expensive. In 1992, the Ford Foundation came to the assistance of Dudley Neighbors with a loan of $2 million, at an annual interest rate of only one percent, giving a great boost to the trust's efforts to acquire and develop land.

To date, about 600 of the 1,300 abandoned parcels have been transformed into homes, gardens, and public spaces.

Affordable Housing

Building affordable housing is the core mission of Dudley Neighbors, and their efforts are paying off. Winthrop Estates, the first affordable housing development, was completed by 1994 and consists of 36 semi-detached, three-bedroom homes, for families at or above an $18,000 annual income. The units cost $150,000 to build but sold for only $90,000. Stafford Heights, a 41-unit cooperative, is even more affordable-suitable for families earning $15,000 or more. It is a mix of two-, three-, and four-bedroom row houses, duplexes, and triplexes.

The two developments follow smart-growth design principles with compact lots that make efficient use of land, classic city sidewalks that encourage walking, and narrow streets that keep traffic at safe speeds. Houses also feature front porches, which helps foster community. The streets are lively, with children racing in front of the houses and people calling out to one another.

At this point, over 350 new units of affordable housing have been built for the Dudley neighborhood, and a comparable number has been rehabilitated by community development corporations, developers, and private homeowners. Some of this development took place on land leased by the neighborhood trust; yet more was inspired by the neighborhood's overall progress. In 2000, the Fannie Mae Foundation named the Dudley Street area one of the nation's ten most promising urban neighborhoods for affordable homeownership and capital investment.

More Than the Sum of Its Parts

From the outset, DSNI has been a strong champion of its community's interests. In addition to its work on housing and environmental cleanup, the initiative campaigned to reopen Roxbury's train station, which had closed in 1986 as a result of the elimination of transit service on Roxbury's orange line. Because the neighborhood was left with only limited bus service to downtown, DSNI lobbied the Massachusetts Bay Transportation Authority to add a neighborhood stop to a commuter train running through the community. In 1987, the station was reopened, providing residents with the link they needed. The initiative also facilitated the creation of a diverse set of community gardens and parks, as well as a beautiful town common. And it helped wrest Mary Hannon Park from drug dealers by establishing a regular program of ongoing youth activities and sports in the park.

DSNI also helped establish an annual neighborhood cleanup, a multicultural festival, and a youth summer program. In 1998, Community Academy, a high school for 14-to-22 year-olds, moved into the neighborhood. In 1999, ground was broken for a community center. An urban agriculture program, which currently features a farmers market supplied partly by the neighborhood's community gardens, will soon be expanded with the building of a year-round greenhouse.

But this path-breaking community venture is more than the sum of its achievements. It demonstrates that members of a diverse community—youthful and elderly, unemployed and employed, of all ethnic backgrounds—can work together to improve their destiny. It shows that a community can combine its own human capital with available outside resources to build a vision. It shows the value of long-term planning and persistence. Ultimately, the continuing success of the Dudley Street Neighborhood Initiative stems from the power of bringing together a diverse community to dream and act.

MCI CENTER
WASHINGTON, D.C.

Only a few years ago, the area that is today the "new downtown" of Washington, D.C. was a run-down, forgotten part of the city's old downtown. Littered with vacant lots and buildings, it was where drug traders went about their business and few outsiders ventured after dark. Today, the whole area is transformed: brand-new office buildings line the streets, hotels and new restaurants are opening their doors, and construction sites announce the arrival of new apartments, entertainment venues, and shops. At the heart of the transformation is a $220 million, one-million-square-feet, glass and stone multiuse sports arena: the MCI Center.

TRANSIT-ORIENTED ARENA REVITALIZES DOWNTOWN

Suburbs and City Compete for New Arena

In 1973, Abe Pollin, the longtime owner of two of Washington's professional sports franchises—the National Basketball Association's Wizards and the National Hockey League's Capitals—built the teams' previous home in the Maryland suburbs. The Capital Centre (later named USAir Arena) was a typical suburban facility, accessible only by car. When it turned 20, Pollin decided it was time to build a new, state-of-the-art facility.

Maryland and Virginia officials approached Pollin with lucrative deals, offering large public subsidies for the new arena. But he wanted to build in downtown Washington. It made sense to choose a central location served by all the area's Metrorail transit lines and near corporations that would pay for luxury suites, club seats, and other corporate services. On the other hand, in the early 1990s, Washington, D.C. was in bad financial shape.

Dusk falls on the MCI Center.

JAMES E. MCLAUGHLIN IV

Suffering from a lingering perception of crime, the city had a bad reputation among the many suburban fans of the two teams. Still,

SMART-GROWTH FEATURES
- ▶ Replaced automobile-dependent arena in suburbs
- ▶ Built atop major rail transit hub
- ▶ Shopping and entertainment functions enliven the area all day long
- ▶ Greatly boosted investor confidence in downtown
- ▶ Catalyst for area's redevelopment

Pollin placed his bets on the downtown location. In doing so, he was not only guided by a forward-looking business sense, telling him that better times were ahead for Washington, but also by a genuine desire to help the city.

This sense of dedication kept Pollin at the table for two years of complicated negotiations, involving multiple city agencies and a bloated city bureaucracy. During the negotiations, Washington was sinking deeper and deeper into debt. In the end, the city government could not deliver the initially promised public subsidy. Pollin chose to build the arena downtown anyway, with his own money.

Even though it could not make a financial commitment, the city did offer support. It donated the land, paid for expensive site preparations, fast-tracked the project, and cut red tape. Business leaders and downtown advocates also provided significant support for the project.

Once the city and Pollin reached a final agreement in 1996, construction proceeded quickly. It took only 19 months to build the MCI Center—a record for a facility of its size—even with such challenges as building above a multilevel Metro rail transit station and having to reroute a high-security communication line serving the White House at a cost of $4 million.

A Convenient, Accessible Arena

Although some suburbanites worried initially about safety at the new location, most fans have followed their teams downtown. In addition to the Wizards and the Capitals, the Hoyas, Georgetown University's basketball team, moved to the arena. In 1998, they were joined by the Women's National Basketball Association's Mystics. The MCI Center has also at-

MCI CENTER FACTS
- ▶ 1 million square feet
- ▶ 20,000 seats
- ▶ 110 luxury suites
- ▶ $220 million construction cost
- ▶ About 200 events a year

tracted new patrons who find the downtown location more convenient than the previous suburban location. Games at the MCI Center begin at 7:00 P.M., a half-hour earlier than they did at USAir Arena, to encourage downtown employees to head directly to the games after work. Corporate sponsors, who pay up to $175,000 annually for the luxury suites, also find this starting time more convenient. In 2001, the arena hosted the National Basketball Association's showcase All-Star game and extravaganza.

The MCI Center's location is one of its greatest assets. It is close not only to downtown businesses, but also to Washington's convention center, and it is within walking distance of the National Mall and its world-class galleries, museums, and historic and civic monuments. The National Museum of American Art and the National Portrait Gallery are located only one block to the west; Chinatown offers restaurants to the north. Both the flag atop the White House and the statue of Freedom on the Capitol dome are visible from the MCI Center, giving the arena a distinctly Washingtonian identity.

PRINCIPALS

Developer: Abe Pollin
Design: Ellerbe Beckett Architects
Public sector: Office of the Mayor, District of Columbia; DC Redevelopment Land Agency
Other: National Capital Development Corp.; Federal City Council; DC Chamber of Commerce

It is particularly significant to smart growth that the MCI Center is the focal point of an extensive and heavily used regional transportation system. The arena sits directly above Metrorail's Gallery Place subway station, where the yellow, red, and green lines meet, and it is only a couple of blocks from stations that serve the blue and orange lines. An estimated 50 to 60 percent of the audience at large MCI Center events uses public transportation, according to several surveys—an amount that surpasses expectations. In fact, Metro must run extra trains on game nights. The MCI Center's location thus helps to eliminate thousands of automobile trips at every game, providing a major environmental benefit for a region with significant air pollution.

A Shopping, Cultural, and Entertainment Complex

Like many arenas, the MCI Center is a multiuse facility, hosting concerts and special events on nights with no games. But it also houses a sports museum with interactive exhibits, two restaurants, and a sporting goods store. These venues ensure that the arena enlivens its environment

DOWNTOWN D.C. TODAY

▶ $3 billion in development projects
▶ 5,000 new employees in last two years
▶ 7.9 million visitors in 1998
▶ 72 percent hotel occupancy
▶ $65 million capital improvement program

not only on game and show nights, but all day, every day.

In fact, the MCI Center was built on land that had once been home to a vibrant downtown shopping area, but which had fallen into neglect after the riots following the 1968 murder of Martin Luther King, Jr., sent businesses fleeing to the suburbs. Although downtown had begun to rebound in the 1980s, most of the new development was farther west, leaving the old downtown retail district derelict.

The MCI Center was the catalyst that reversed the fortunes of this area, which today is once again one of the hottest office and retail markets in the city. Abe Pollin's decision to build his new arena there dramatically boosted investors' confidence in the surrounding area. A business improvement district was formed to create an attractive and sustainable business environment. These developments took place in the midst of a period of strong local and national economic growth, during which the area saw the construction and renovation of office buildings, entertainment and retail venues, and even some downtown housing.

The success of the MCI Center is testament to many things, but none is more important than the commitment and vision of Abe Pollin to his city. Smart growth needs heroes and, as Pollin shows, sometimes one person can make a difference.

The Downtown DC BID (Business Improvement District) serves a 110-block neighborhood, containing approximately 825 properties. Its signature corps of 80 SAMs provides cleaning and maintenance services and serve as eyes and ears for local law enforcement agencies and as guides to visitors. In addition, two social workers establish contact with homeless people and refer them to an innovative center that provides multiple services. The Downtown DC BID has also been working with the city to implement a physical improvement program

SNAPSHOT: DOWNTOWN DC BUSINESS IMPROVEMENT DISTRICT

Business Improvement Districts (BIDs) have benefited a number of downtowns around the country. In a BID, businesses tax themselves to pay for such district-wide improvements as cleanup, maintenance, safety, streetscape beautification, and transportation services.

On November 17, 1997, two weeks before Washington, D.C.'s, new sports arena, the MCI Center opened, the Downtown DC Business Improvement District launched its services. Safety And Maintenance workers (SAMs), clad in bright red uniforms, took to the streets to collect trash, remove graffiti, and restore a sense of order before the first game brought thousands of visitors to the area. Since then, the MCI Center and the Downtown DC BID have enjoyed a symbiotic relationship—each benefiting from the activities of the other, and jointly inspiring confidence in both citizens and businesses in the resurgence of downtown.

that includes brighter and more attractive street lights, better signs, upgraded sidewalks, and new street furniture and landscaping.

Working with the regional transit agency, the DC BID has also been encouraging visitors to use Metro and has helped extend its hours of operation. Two circulating bus routes that would connect the area with the National Mall are now being planned. Under the guidance of a board of directors made up mainly of local property owners, a small professional staff administers these programs and markets the area to tourists, local residents, and businesses.

While the MCI Center has boosted the viability of the area and has attracted tens of thousands of sport fans and visitors downtown, Downtown DC BID has provided the order, cleanliness, infrastructure, and marketing necessary for sustained growth. According to Seamus Houston, director of marketing and communications of the DC BID, "We now have a new sense of community among the district's property owners, who acknowledge responsibility for the area's problems, take pride in the area's successes, and share a vision for its future."

PULASKI STATION
CHICAGO, ILLINOIS

The story of Pulaski Station is really two success stories in one: how an urban neighborhood decided to use its mass transit station as a catalyst for community development, and

COMMUNITY CALLS FOR TRANSIT-ORIENTED REDEVELOPMENT

how a transit line serving almost 15,000 people a day was saved from being permanently shut down.

Public Transit in Jeopardy

The Lake Street Elevated Line (El) runs from Chicago's Loop to suburban Oak Park, through the heart of Chicago's west side. In many of these neighborhoods, especially those in the city, shrinking populations and declining economic activity led to a decrease in El ridership in recent decades. The problem was exacerbated by a declining quality of service, as years of neglect caused deterioration of tracks and stations. The Chicago Transit Authority (CTA) combined the Lake Street El with another line in 1993, and then proposed to close down the consolidated "green line" altogether, arguing that repairs would be too costly. At the time of the CTA's announcement, 118,000 people,

Rendering of Pulaski Commercial Center.

FARR ASSOCIATES ARCHITECTURE & URBAN DESIGN

many without cars, were living within a half-mile of the
Lake Street El tracks.

One of the stations that
would have been abandoned
and eventually demolished
was Pulaski Station in the
West Garfield neighborhood. The neighborhood had many assets: a
viable commercial and shopping strip, some industry, and many
important community institutions. But its predominantly African-
American residents were far removed from the prosperity of the city,
even though the neighborhood was only three miles from the downtown Loop. Once a solid industrial, wholesale, and warehouse area,
West Garfield fell on hard times after devastating riots in the 1960s
and 1970s. Investors fled, and many industrial and retail sites became
vacant. The population declined from 60,000 in 1950 to just 24,000
in 1990; those who remained tended to have low incomes.

Living standards were particularly low for the 2,700 people living
within the four city blocks closest to the station, where average per
capita annual income was just $6,708. Fewer than half of those resi-
dents owned a car. Moreover, before the revitalization effort began, 40
percent of all land stood vacant in this four-block area. The neighborhood looked "bombed out," as one resident put it. And, while
around 2,000 people got on and off the El at Pulaski Station every
day, the station was overlooked as a potential community resource
and focal point. Fortunately, that was about to change.

Saving the Green Line

The potential loss of transit service galvanized the community. To save
the green line, a broad collection of inner-city and suburban interests,
including the Center for Neighborhood Technology, formed the Lake
Street El Coalition. As coalition members lobbied the CTA, they
thought about ways to increase ridership and to harvest maximum
benefit from the line for the neighborhoods. Transit-oriented development (TOD)—intensifying housing and commercial activity
around transit stations (see Glossary)—promised to be a win-win idea
for both CTA and the neighborhoods. Pulaski Station was soon to
become Chicago's first model TOD.

Plans materialized quickly for redevelopment of the Pulaski Station
neighborhood. The coalition coordinated a series of community meet-

PRINCIPALS

Developer: Bethel New Life, Inc.
Design: Farr Associates Architecture & Urban Design
Other: Center for Neighborhood Technology

ings, with technical help from Farr Associates, a local architecture and urban design firm that provided much of its assistance to the community on a pro bono basis. In these meetings, called charettes, residents agreed on a series of development objectives: improved pedestrian access to the station; 24-hour commercial activity and police presence at the station; infill housing and rehabilitation; retail and commercial revitalization; and the retention and creation of industrial activity within walking distance from the station. The coalition presented CTA with drawings, plans, and proposed specifications to meet these objectives.

The coalition did its work very well indeed. Only ten days after the Lake Street El Coalition unveiled plans for Pulaski Station, CTA announced a reversal in its plans for the green line. CTA pledged a $300 million investment, both to reconstruct the elevated structure and to build new stations along the line, including a mixed-use "superstation" at Pulaski.

Bethel New Life, a community organization whose roots lay in the neighborhood's Bethel Lutheran Church, coordinated most of the on-the-ground redevelopment effort in the Pulaski Station neighborhood. Bethel New Life was committed to involving the community in the process. Drawing upon the environmental expertise of the Center for Neighborhood Technology, it also brought a number of environmental goals to the table: energy-efficient housing in a compact configuration; traffic-calming strategies; brownfields cleanup and redevelopment; and a business strategy that emphasized bringing environmental and other jobs into the community.

Social and Environmental Benefits

As of this writing, almost one hundred affordable, energy-efficient homes have been built within walking distance of the station, and another hundred are planned. Pocket parks and traffic calming devices have been created for the enjoyment, safety, and comfort of local residents. A grocery store has opened a block from the station, and a commercial bank will open soon. New jobs have been created by attracting a large moving and storage company, which employs 250 people, to the area and by cleaning up a two-acre site and building a recycling plant that trains and employs many local residents. Cleanup of additional properties is underway.

Partly as a result of repeated turnovers in its top management, CTA has been slow to deliver its superstation plan for Pulaski Station. The agency remains committed, however, and the adjacent areas, which fall under Bethel New Life's management, are in the process of being developed: Phase I will include a 23,000-square-foot commercial center, housing a day-care facility, a health clinic, and other businesses. This will be an energy-efficient building constructed with recycled materials, and it will feature photovoltaic and fuel cells and a roof

SNAPSHOT: **SMART GROWTH AND GLOBAL WARMING**

With sprawl development, automobile and freight delivery trips get longer as origins and destinations are spread out farther and farther from each other. Sprawl also makes the use of alternatives such as walking and taking public transit less and less convenient for commuting to work or school, as well as for practical errands such as shopping or going out to eat. The result is that, as a nation, we are driving our vehicles more often and farther each year; total miles driven nationwide increased by an astounding 68 percent between 1980 and 1997.

This means that we are burning more and more gasoline and diesel fuel each year. As an inevitable consequence of increasing fossil fuel combustion, we are releasing more and more greenhouse gases, especially carbon dioxide, into the atmosphere. More than a third—and the fastest-growing portion—of U.S. greenhouse gases come from the transportation sector, with carbon dioxide emissions from transportation growing steadily by about two percent per year in the 1990s. With only five percent of the world's population, the U.S. is responsible for about one-fifth of global carbon dioxide emissions annually.

These trends do not bode well for planetary health. There is now a strong scientific consensus that greenhouse gases, which accumulate and remain in the atmosphere for exceptionally long times, are causing the earth's surface temperature to rise, melting the polar ice caps and causing sea level to rise. The Intergovernmental Panel on Climate Change, an organization involving scientists from 120 nations, predicts that the consequences could eventually include serious health risks from increased heat waves and the spread of tropical and vector-borne diseases, severe flooding in coastal areas, and major disruption of water flows, forests, agriculture, and the world's ecosystems.

Smart growth can help. By reducing the need to drive and the distances covered when we do, smart-growth neighborhoods generate reduced carbon dioxide emissions compared to sprawling developments. EPA research on Atlanta's Atlantic Station development, discussed earlier, indicates that it will generate 58 and 62 percent less carbon dioxide than would two conventional outer-suburban developments of the same interior square footage. The research also found that Atlantic Station will produce 22 percent less carbon dioxide than would a closer-in suburban development covering the same land area, but with significantly inferior transit service and mixed-use amenities.[12]

garden. This commercial center will be connected to the station's elevated platform. Also directly accessible from the transit stop will be a mixed-use development with residential and commercial spaces that will be built in the second phase of construction.

Community members believe these changes have benefited their neighborhood tremendously. The development of Pulaski Station as a model TOD has helped bring a diversity of funds and technical assistance into the community and energized the local residents and their community associations. Less tangible but perhaps more important, the revitalization has given people a new sense of hope and pride in their neighborhood.

Planners believe the TOD will also meet its goal of boosting ridership on the El. Transportation forecasts for Pulaski Station have shown that vehicle trips are likely to decline and be replaced by transit and walking. The Chicago chapter of the American Lung Association has estimated that the Pulaski Station plan will eliminate 17.5 percent of neighborhood vehicle trips to work and 20 percent of all other neighborhood vehicle trips, saving 1,556 miles of vehicle travel every day or 567,940 miles per year.

This translates into reduced emissions of carbon dioxide—the principal greenhouse gas that causes global warming—and significant air quality improvements, including a reduction in emissions of the key precursors for ozone smog. Emissions of volatile organic compounds are expected to decline annually by 7.6 tons and nitrogen oxides by 3.04 tons. These projected improvements have

qualified the Green Line project for federal financial assistance through the Congestion Mitigation and Air Quality (CMAQ) program established under federal transportation legislation. The CMAQ funds will be used to support further planning of the Pulaski Station area and to replicate the area's success at three additional stations along the Green Line.

QUALITY HILL

KANSAS CITY, KANSAS

The bluff that overlooks the city's emerging business district on one side and the broad Missouri River on the other was once home to the most prestigious neighborhood in Kansas City. Called Quality Hill by the envious, it was home to the city's early leaders, begin-

MIXED-INCOME HOUSING RESTORES NEIGHBORHOOD'S FORMER GLORY

ning with its first mayor, Johnston Lykins, who built the first home there in 1856.

Victorian mansions and elegant brick townhouses followed. The plush Coates House, with its marble staircase, ornate lobby, and Turkish baths, served as Quality Hill's trademark hotel.

When stockyards and slaughterhouses were built on land below the bluff at the turn of the twentieth century, the area began to decline. As the wealthy fled from the offending odors, the old mansions were converted into boarding houses and apartments for laborers and servants. Although the stockyards were removed after World War II, the

Affordable housing in Quality Hill.

deterioration continued, in large part driven by the migration of people and businesses from the city to the suburbs. By the early 1980s, Quality Hill was in an advanced state of decay: buildings were used primarily by transient renters, and many were damaged by fire and neglect.

Area Slated for Rehabilitation

Recognizing that residential development was important for creating round-the-clock activity downtown, Kansas City's leaders invited McCormack, Baron & Associates, a St. Louis development company that specialized in inner-city, mixed-income housing, to evaluate nearby potential sites. Richard Baron, one of the company's principals, was attracted by the distinctive location and historic architecture of Quality Hill.

MCCORMACK BARON

In order to reshape the image of the run-down neighborhood and attract new residents, a critical mass of transformation was needed. This required that a large-enough area—five blocks for just the first phase of construction—be assembled. Negotiations proved difficult, involving absentee landlords and land speculators as well as individual homeowners. The city helped to acquire properties and, where deteriorated structures had to be razed, paid relocation expenses for affected households and businesses. A few owners held out, but most of those who did undertook renovations on their own once the revitalization effort got underway.

While assembling the initial development site was a challenge, raising sufficient investment became even more difficult. A projected gap of $29 million between the amount of debt available for the project under usual lending standards and its projected cost had to be filled with grants and creative financing. Federal historic tax credits and low-income housing credits were helpful, but insufficient.

McCormack, Baron forged an unprecedented public-private partnership to secure the resources to renovate the existing structures, build new ones, and install historically accurate improvements. On the private side, local banks, businesses, foundations, and a New York brokerage house provided the first and second mortgage debt and equity. On the public side, the project received federal, state and city support in the form of grants for public improvements and tax abatement. Each funding source provided additional leverage for obtaining further support.

Renovation and New Construction

In 1985, after three difficult years of negotiations, construction began. The first phase of the project comprised 23 buildings, 13 of which were historic restorations. Rebuilt facades, replaced gables and turrets, and remodeled roofs returned the buildings to their original appearance, while new plumbing and wiring brought modern-day conveniences. Ten of the 13 historic buildings were remodeled for residential use. Some feature apartments, while others are divided into attached townhouses and garden flats.

The other three have been converted to commercial uses. The Progress Club, built in 1893 as a Jewish social club, has been leased to the YMCA for use as a health club and meeting facility. The Virginia Hotel, built in 1877, now houses the Missouri Industrial Development Commission. And the famous Coates House has been extensively remodeled and restored to its former grandeur. The upper floors have been converted to apartments, while the street level contains shops and offices.

Quality Hill's new structures, built of red brick in Victorian and Colonial styles, blend in with the restored ones. Decorative streetlights, new sidewalks, curbs, median strips, gutters, and street plantings further reinforce the historic nature of the area and make the streets inviting to pedestrians. The city spent more than $2 million on these street improvements. Today, with its beautifully restored historic buildings blending in with sensitive new construction, its great views of the river and the city, and its proximity to a vibrant downtown, the new Quality Hill is once again a sought-after address.

A Mix of Incomes and Lifestyles

Quality Hill is not exclusively an address for the wealthy, as it once was. As with all their projects, McCormack, Baron set aside some of the units for low-income families, while they rent others at market rate. Today, with all three phases of the Quality Hill redevelopment complete, 493 residential units have been created. One-fifth of these are reserved for households at 80 percent of the area's median income, and an additional allocation is set aside for households at 60 percent. The subsidized units are indistinguishable from the market-rate ones and are distributed throughout the neighborhood.

PRINCIPALS

Developer: McCormack Baron and Associates, Inc.
Design: Peckham Guyton Albers& Viets, Inc.
Public sector: City of Kansas City
Other: Hall Family Foundation

The rebuilt, reconceived Quality Hill has become a market success. Ninety-eight percent of the apartments are leased. Residents come from all walks of life, but concentrations of single professionals, young couples, and older people are particularly high. Some work only a short walk away in the central business district, but others work within the boundaries of the Quality Hill neighborhood, which attracted several large office tenants in the 1990s. Interestingly, even people who work in the suburbs choose to live here, because of Quality Hill's unique historic and urban character.

A large number of the first residents came from out of town but, as the image of Quality Hill has changed in the eyes of locals, more and more people have moved in from other parts of the city and from the suburbs. In fact, in a 1998 survey, Quality Hill was rated by downtown workers as the most desirable of the city's nearby neighborhoods.

Quality Hill is not a perfect smart-growth neighborhood. There is a shortage of neighborhood services, which forces people to drive for shopping and other errands. And, while bus lines serve the area, transit is not necessarily a convenient, widely used option. Those who do not work within walking distance of downtown are likely to drive their cars to work, although driving distances are shorter to city destinations than they are for suburban residents.

Nevertheless, Quality Hill is a success story. The mix of incomes makes it unusual and provides an alternative to both gentrification and the isolation of the poor. Moreover, Quality Hill's redevelopment not only has restored the neighborhood to its former glory but also demonstrates the feasibility and advantages of living in and near downtown. Altogether, some ten thousand people now choose to reside in and around downtown Kansas City.

RUTLAND WAL-MART
RUTLAND, VERMONT

"Vermont is just plain beautiful," claims the state's official website. "Vermont kept its landscape open, productive, fresh and pristine . . . the scale is small and intimate here."

Can a string of Wal-Mart stores and their enormous parking lots, as big as ten football fields, fit into this idyllic landscape? We all know what typical big-box stores look like (windowless, expansive boxes fronted by a sea of asphalt), where they tend to locate (at the very edge of small towns, in places accessible only by car), and what effect they can have on a town's small businesses (many are driven out of business or are forced to move, decimating downtown life). So it might not be surprising to learn that Vermont was named one of America's 11 Most Endangered Places by the National Trust for Historic Preservation in 1993, after Wal-Mart announced its plans to open several new stores around the state.

EVEN A BIG-BOX CHAIN CAN GO DOWNTOWN

But there is a surprising and hopeful aspect of Wal-Mart's entry into the state: the corporate giant agreed to make substantial changes to its store locations and design in several, though not all, Vermont locations. The Rutland store is a particularly inspiring example of how a big chain—and one particularly vilified for practices that promote sprawl—can provide its services and meet its business needs without weakening a traditional downtown and converting a greenfield into parking lots at the edge of town.

Wal-Mart shopping center in downtown Rutland.

A Dialogue Begins
Vermont's "endangered" status was widely publicized, and it sparked extensive debate about the pros and cons

of Wal-Mart's entry into the state. Many Vermonters feared that the advent of huge stores would cause irreparable harm to the state's character and their way of life. Others felt that Wal-Mart's arrival would provide needed jobs and discounted products. The disagreement was especially sharp in towns with struggling economies. Vermont's governor, Howard Dean, was particularly concerned. In the fall of 1993, he met with executives of the Wal-Mart Company to express his hope that it would support the state's efforts to protect its downtowns and legendary countryside.

SMART-GROWTH FEATURES

- ► Downtown location
- ► Reuse of an existing building
- ► Shared parking
- ► Design adjustments for a better local fit
- ► Fruitful public/private/nonprofit cooperation

Wal-Mart's plans also worried Paul Bruhn, executive director of the Preservation Trust of Vermont. He knew that, in many other states, Wal-Mart's arrival had caused the decline of older downtowns, the abandonment of beautiful historic buildings, and a profound change in the character of the affected communities. Bruhn got a chance to convey his concerns to Wal-Mart's vice president for corporate affairs, Donald E. Shinkle, in a July 1994 program hosted by Vermont Public Radio. He explained that Vermont preservationists did not oppose Wal-Mart per se; what they opposed was sprawl. If Wal-Mart would build projects that reinforced Vermont's existing communities, local preservationists would work with, not against, the company. Bruhn asked Shinkle if he would arrange for key Wal-Mart officials to come to Vermont and tour several downtowns with him. Bruhn wanted to demonstrate that there were, in fact, viable downtown locations for the company's stores if they were scaled down to fit the size of Vermont's communities. Shinkle said yes.

A month later, seven people toured the downtowns of three cities: St. Albans, Burlington, and Rutland. Wal-Mart sent three representatives, including its executive vice president for real estate and its New England representative, Sandra Watson. Representing the preservation advocates was Bruhn, an aide to Governor Dean, and an architect experienced in working with big-box retailers. The entourage also included a politically influential Burlington lawyer.

The tours helped each side gain a better understanding of the other's perspective. The preservationists learned about Wal-Mart's parking and traffic-management needs. The Wal-Mart representatives saw how vibrant the downtowns were, and became intrigued by the possibilities in downtown Rutland and Burlington. Rutland had room for a store with approximately 75,000 square feet, while Burlington had room for a store with 100,000 square feet; both cities could provide adequate parking. Wal-Mart showed little interest in downtown St. Albans, however, partly because the company had already started the application process to build a typical sprawl-type store at the town's edge, and also because the downtown site would have presented parking and traffic-flow challenges.

Watson followed up with Bruhn, and the two discussed possible locations in Rutland, Burlington, and Bennington, which Wal-Mart scouted out on its own. They agreed to disagree about St. Albans.

In September 1995, less than a year after the tour of the three cities, Wal-Mart opened the Bennington store—its first in Vermont—in a recycled Woolworth building. Though not located in Bennington's downtown, the store was nonetheless a major step in the right direction. At only 52,000 square feet, it was about half the size of typical new Wal-Marts, and it fit better with the small scale of a Vermont town. The store reused existing retail space, and it did not create new sprawl in the countryside.

Downtown Rutland

In the meantime, negotiations over a downtown site in Rutland, a city of 18,000 in central Vermont, began in earnest. They focused on the Rutland Shopping Plaza, a 1960s-era strip shopping center in the middle of the city, right across from the downtown historic district. Kmart, which occupied a large space on the plaza for years, had left, and had recently announced its intention to move to a new mall on the outskirts of town. The 75,000-square-foot space it had vacated, once considered for demolition, was eventually to become the new Wal-Mart store.

SNAPSHOT: **COULD IT BE A TREND?**

In the spring of 2001, another big-box chain, Home Depot, announced a particularly innovative and ambitious plan to invest in an urban location. In particular, the country's third-largest retailer is developing a four-story, mixed-use project in an older, historic section of Portland, Oregon. The four-acre development—Home Depot stores and parking lots usually occupy 15 acres—Halsey Place, will feature a varied, brick façade designed to resemble several adjacent buildings, along with offices, apartments, and parking above the retail space.

Although the Kmart store stood empty when Wal-Mart representatives first looked at the site, there were many signs that the shopping plaza was on the rebound. This renaissance was due to a successful partnership between the city and the private sector. On the public side, city planning and revitalization efforts had begun in the late 1980s, starting with an extensive community planning process. The resulting strategic plan set out to rebuild the downtown as an alternative to sprawl. The city had begun to act on the plan in 1989 and 1990, creating a special assessment district to pay for public improvements downtown.

On the private side, the owner of the plaza, Net Realty Holding Trust, invested in a major renovation and brought in several new tenants, reversing years of declining occupancy. The most significant new tenant was Price Chopper, which committed to open a 58,000 square-foot supermarket, the largest in Vermont. Other tenants followed, including T.J. Maxx, a discount clothier, and Cinema North, a nine-screen cinema complex.

By the time Wal-Mart was brought in to visit Rutland, these and other businesses were already open and doing well. The Rutland Price Chopper ranked among the chain's best performers, and revenues at the T.J. Maxx store exceeded corporate projections by about 30 percent. The success of these businesses demonstrated to Wal-Mart the economic viability of the Rutland Shopping Plaza site.

The efforts of the city, Net Realty Holding Trust, Governor Dean, and the Preservation Trust of Vermont bore fruit on April 25, 1996, when Wal-Mart announced it had signed a long-term lease for the vacant Kmart building.

With the help of a local architectural firm, NFB Architects, Wal-Mart redesigned the building in accordance with the new features of the refurbished plaza as a whole. The firm's design called for red bricks for the exterior façade, and it suggested a green roof reminiscent of the railroad buildings that once occupied the site. NFB also worked to relate the store to the historic district across the street from the plaza. Instead of using a standard sign in its signature colors, Wal-Mart agreed to the white lettering used by other stores in the plaza. The company also agreed to share its parking lot with other local businesses, to minimize the waste of unused parking spaces.

Within nine months of signing the lease, Wal-Mart had navigated the entire local and state permitting process and had renovated and stocked the store. The grand opening took place on January 29, 1999.

The Keys to Success: Leadership, Flexibility, and Cooperation

Several factors lay behind Vermont's success in getting Wal-Mart to go downtown in Rutland. From the start, the project enjoyed inspired leadership from the city, Net Realty Holding Trust, the governor, and the Preservation Trust of Vermont, among others. For example, without the groundwork laid in the late eighties by the city, and without the city's and Net Realty's success in persuading other retailers to come downtown, the downtown would not have held the same attraction for Wal-Mart.

Flexibility on the part of the Wal-Mart Corporation was another key factor. Had the company not accepted Bruhn's tour invitation, and had it not considered the viability of doing business "out of the box," the Rutland store would never have been conceived, much less built.

SNAPSHOT: SMART GROWTH AND SUPERSTORE SPRAWL

In the last decade, big-box superstores have been sprouting up all over the country, often on farmland or meadows at the outer fringes of suburbia. Between 1992 and 1994, 55 percent of all new retail space in America came in the form of big-box superstores; in 1994, 80 percent of all new stores fell into this category.

While these stores sometimes offer welcome convenience and price discounts to shoppers, they can have serious negative impacts on our environment and communities. In particular, because these very large stores use space wastefully and tend to locate in greenfield locations, they lead to unnecessary destruction of farmland, forests, and meadows. Their enormous parking lots become heat islands during warm, sunny weather and cause stormwater runoff and water pollution when it rains. And a single superstore can generate as many as 10,000 car trips per day, as a result of the lack of alternative means of access for customers.

Moreover, superstores can drain the vitality out of older downtowns and displace existing businesses, especially small, locally owned stores. And, at the same time that their presence may lead to the abandonment of beautiful historic buildings, the new superstores' design—as one-story, fortress-like buildings—does not offer much aesthetically. While people may like what's *inside* a superstore, few would find anything appealing about what's on the *outside*.

It is essential for municipalities to consider these consequences of superstores before they rush to provide the new roads, water, and sewer-line extensions, and other subsidies the stores often require. As the Rutland case proves, it is possible even for Wal-Mart to contribute to the revitalization of existing communities rather than to drive sprawl.

Communities that have lacked the leadership and downtown assets that Rutland was able to offer have not fared so well in finding mutually acceptable solutions. Wal-Mart has shown less flexibility in other locations around the state, unfortunately, and the company has run into trouble. For example, Wal-Mart's Williston store, a standard sprawling development, divided that community and was tied up for years in litigation. The controversial out-of-town Wal-Mart in St. Albans was ultimately turned down during Vermont's environmental review process.

But in Rutland, cooperation formed the cornerstone on which the store was built. While the Preservation Trust of Vermont and Wal-Mart could easily have become adversaries under less thoughtful leaders, a cordial relationship was established by identifying common interests and avoiding name-calling. "Instead of just saying no to Wal-Mart, we offered them the alternative of downtown," Bruhn says. "They could finally see that we were not anti-Wal-Mart; we were pro-Vermont downtown, pro-Vermont countryside. In other locations around the country, opponents of Wal-Mart have been branded as 'elitists.' Here, they couldn't put that tag on us because we were actually bending over backwards to help them locate in downtown locations. We succeeded because we offered Wal-Mart the downtown alternative."

Our discussion of the Rutland Wal-Mart and superstore sprawl is based on Constance E. Beaumont's excellent Better Models for Superstores—Alternatives to Big-Box Sprawl, *published by the National Trust for Historic Preservation in 1997.*

SECOND STREET STUDIOS
SANTA FE, NEW MEXICO

Santa Fe, New Mexico, has long been a mecca for artists, artisans, and small businesses. The Southwest city's downtown is teeming with tourists shopping in the numerous galleries and gift shops, and even in the shade of tents that are set up every day in its historic plaza. Just outside of downtown, Canyon **A COMMUNITY OF ARTISTS AND SMALL BUSINESSES** Road is famed for its upscale art galleries. Experiencing these bustling areas, visitors may assume that artists and small businesses are doing very well in Santa Fe.

Some, indeed, are. Most start-up businesses and young artists at the beginning of their careers, however, simply cannot afford to set up shop downtown or on Canyon Road. Forced to locations on the fringe of town, they find it difficult to market their artwork or products.

Santa Fe's Second Street Studios caters to the needs of such young artisans and business owners while following smart-growth principles. It offers a flexible and affordable space in a location that was previously in decline but has now become a Santa Fe destination.

Flexible Design Accommodates Live/Work Arrangements

Second Street Studios was planned and developed by local developers Susan and Wayne Nichols, affordable housing developer Jonathan Rose, and planner Peter Calthorpe. The partners sought to offer maximum flexibility. They designed the two-story buildings so that the ground floor can be used as a studio, shop, or other workspace, while the upstairs can be used either as a residential loft or additional work or storage space. Those residents who create a live/work unit can save the cost of paying for separate living and working

The courtyard and studios at Second Street.

quarters, while enjoying the convenience of "commuting" one flight of stairs. The integrated live/work environment seems to appeal especially to artists, although some service professionals and small business owners have also embraced this lifestyle. Because of the flexible design, it is easy for residents to change the function of the second floor from work or storage space to living area or vice versa.

From the beginning, the developers set affordability as a particular goal. They achieved it by building on relatively low-priced land and by saving on materials whenever possible. In spite of such thriftiness, however, Second Street Studios does not look cheap.

One reason is its innovative, beautiful design. The community is constructed around a series of tree-filled courtyards. The lush, sunlight-filled courtyards soften and enrich the look of the buildings surrounding them. They also lend a local flavor by suggesting the classic form of a New Mexico marketplace plaza. Attractive wooden walkways give access to the second floor, and bright colors lend a dynamic touch.

In addition to being attractive, Second Street Studios also harbors a number of environmentally sensitive features. For instance, it takes advantage of New Mexico's sunny climate with floors that retain and then radiate solar heat. It also makes maximum use of natural daylight, while sunshading devices keep out excess heat on hot summer days. In addition, a community-wide recycling program has been put in place, and water-saving devices are installed in all toilets and showers.

Given the high demand for the units over the years, rents in Second Street Studios have risen from the original bargain price of $7 per square foot. But they are still very competitive, at $9.50 to $14 per square foot.

A One-of-a-Kind Community Develops

Builders completed the first phase of the construction in just six months, in 1990. In spite of minimal advertising, the developers leased more than half of the 35 units on opening. The remaining units were leased within two months. Today, the whole five-acre site is built and all 70 units are occupied.

From the beginning, Second Street Studios attracted a diverse mix containing artists, craftspeople, and small, sometimes unorthodox businesses. The initial tenant roster included: photographers; painters; sculptors; a glass blower; holistic healing practitioners; a toy inventor; a caterer; a fine art printing company; clothing, jewelry, textile, and computer software designers; and aikido and yoga centers. Over the years, some artists and businesses have "graduated" from Second Street Studios and moved on, with new ones taking their place. But the overall mix has remained diverse. Heather Heimerl of Santa Fe Glassworks summed the spirit of the complex to *The New Mexican:* "I think it has all the best of a community—like-minded people with similar interests. It's an opportunity for everyone to complement each other."[13]

The combination of studios and businesses offers a lot to see, do, and buy without leaving Second Street Studios. Instead of driving, visitors can accomplish a number of errands on foot. And, if they get hungry after all the shopping, classes, and gallery-hopping available at this development, they need only cross the street to find a popular bakery and a pub. When people do drive, they tend to travel relatively short distances, since the development is only two miles from Santa Fe's historic downtown plaza.

Although Second Street Studios is next to a recently reactivated rail line, the trains do not currently stop at the development. Tenants and neighborhood activists have been campaigning for a permanent train stop. But those who like to bicycle do not need to wait to gain easy access to and from Second Street Studios. A bike trail runs parallel with the rail line and provides a safe and easy route from the development to Santa Fe's downtown and other points.

New Construction, Old Neighborhood

Second Street Studios is among the first newly constructed live/work projects since the Great Depression of the 1930s. But, while the buildings are new, they are located in an old neighborhood, between

SNAPSHOT: **SMART GROWTH AND LIVE/WORK SPACES**

Live/work arrangements tend to have two significant smart-growth features: they eliminate the need to commute to work, and they typically use less land than separate residential and work areas. They offer the additional benefit of creating "24-hour neighborhoods" that remain active both day and night.

an industrial area to the east and a blue-collar barrio to the west. The development has helped to revitalize this overlooked part of Santa Fe and boost its image in the community.

PROJECT DATA
- ▶ 5 acres
- ▶ 70 units
- ▶ Most between 1,200–2,228 sq. ft., some with 600 sq. ft.

As one long-time neighbor, Ed Archuleta, put it: "There is a lot of new energy and excitement in the neighborhood now. A lot of young people, creative people, interesting people are coming here, because of Second Street Studios. For the first time I can remember, our neighborhood is seen as a destination by Santa Feans."

SOUTHSIDE PARK COHOUSING
SACRAMENTO, CALIFORNIA

Approaching Southside Park Cohousing from the street, one sees a block of pretty, colorful, neo-Victorian townhouses with front porches framed by lush green vines and flowerpots. It is a bright spot in the neighborhood, but one that blends in with the scale and style of older houses. Only on entering the complex does one notice that this is more than an especially attractive townhouse develop-

A COOPERATIVE COMMUNITY IN THE CITY

ment. The houses are oriented around a communal green area, featuring a playground. Small, well-tended community gardens thrive in the open space. And a "common house" features meeting and recreation rooms, a large kitchen, and a dining room where residents meet for dinner a few times a week.

A Community of Homeowners

Southside Park Cohousing combines private ownership of housing units with shared community resources for its members. Although the development has been created and run by community consensus, it is far from a commune. The families privately own all units, cars, and other property, and all forms of sharing and attendance at community events are voluntary.

Designed according to the wishes of its owners, Southside Park ful-

Relaxation and play in Southside Park Cohousing.

fills many functions: it revitalizes a neighborhood, offers affordable housing, and provides a safe and sociable place to bring up children—all in a compact, in-town development.

The cohousing concept emerged in Denmark in the 1960s and was introduced to the United States in the late 1980s by architects Kathryn McCamant and Charles Durrett. In their

book, *Cohousing,* they describe what they saw in Denmark as "a new housing type that redefines the concept of neighborhood to fit contemporary lifestyles . . . housing that combines the autonomy of private dwellings with the advantages of community living." Although the cohousing concept is clearly not for everyone, it has attracted a number of Americans. As of this writing, more than a hundred cohousing communities have been completed or are in development across the United States.

SMART-GROWTH FEATURES

▶ Infill development in an inner-city neighborhood
▶ Jobs, shops, entertainment, and transit within walking or biking distance
▶ Successful public-private partnership
▶ Low- and moderate-income units mixed with market-rate units
▶ Neighborhood revitalization

McCamant and Durrett gave a slide show about the cohousing concept in Sacramento in November 1988. Their presentation inspired a number of groups to form, including one that called itself "the Downscalers," which was interested in settling near the city's downtown. The Downscalers hired a project manager and consultant with downtown development experience, David Mogavero, to help them research promising downtown locations. One site in particular, owned by the Sacramento Housing Redevelopment Agency, provided a good fit. The group spent months studying the location and, by the time the redevelopment agency issued a request for proposals to develop it, they were ready to act.

Winning With the Neighborhood's Support

Even though the cohousing concept met many of the criteria requested by the redevelopment agency—such as housing for a range of incomes, and buildings with respect for the scale and character of the existing neighborhood—winning the competition for the site was not easy. In particular, a competing proposal by an out-of-town developer who wanted to build conventional condominiums was initially favored by the agency. The support of neighbors tipped the scales in cohousing's favor.

One of the cohousing group's families had already lived in the neighborhood, while others made a point of making themselves visible and helpful. They participated in neighborhood cleanup days and in the traditional Fourth of July picnic; they talked with neighborhood activists about their ideas. While these gestures did not eliminate suspicions about a group of outsiders moving into their community (it would take many more years to gain genuine trust), the neighbors came to believe that a productive dialogue was more likely with the cohous-

ing residents than with the unknown developers and future residents of the proposed condominiums. Residents of the neighborhood, represented by two people on the redevelopment agency's selection committee, eventually came out in favor of the Downscalers.

Nevertheless, because of the difficulty in getting construction financing for such an unorthodox project, the final approval from the city took two years, from 1990 to 1992. Once the city granted approval, construction proceeded relatively quickly, with a move-in date of late 1993—five years after the original cohousing slide show took place. The happy culmination of the project inspired several original songs, such as this one, set to the old show tune "There's No Business Like Show Business:" "There is no housing like cohousing/Like no housing we know/Everything about it is appealing/Common house and all the units too/ We designed it all from floor to ceiling/And now we're seeing our dreams come true."

PRINCIPALS
Developer: Ergo (assisted by the original residents)
Design and Project Management: Mogavero Notestine Associates
Public sector: City of Sacramento

Affordability and Safety

In spite of the frustrations and delays, working with the city had distinct advantages, most notably in financing low- and moderate-income units. The redevelopment agency recycled half the money it received for the land into subsidized second mortgages for households with qualifying income levels. These mortgages cover up to 49 percent of the cost of the home, and they are held interest-free for the first 30 years for low-income residents and 15 years for moderate-income residents. During this time, no payments are required on these so-called "silent" mortgages. In effect, lower-income families could purchase the already reasonably priced units for almost half the price. Eleven of the 25 households took advantage of the alternative financing. All Southside Park Cohousing residents can also save money on transportation. Living downtown, within walking or close driving distance from jobs, shopping and entertainment, enables residents to spend less on gasoline and automobile maintenance costs, or even reduce the number of cars in their households.

PROJECT DATA
25 homes:
▶ 6 one- and two-bedroom flats
▶ 19 townhouses from two to four bedrooms
A diverse community:
▶ Ages 2-76
▶ 40 adults
▶ 28 children full or part-time
▶ 2 extended families
▶ 5 non-white or multiracial households
Figures as of April 2000.

Southside Park Cohousing has also helped the neighborhood deal with a longstanding crime problem. Even though drug deals still take place daily in the surrounding neighborhood that was once Sacramento's red light district, the cohousing development's residents feel secure without gates, locks, or fences protecting the 25-house complex. Since people have different schedules, with some retired or working from their homes, there are eyes all day long on the centrally located communal areas and the houses that are clustered closely around it. No serious crimes have been committed on cohousing grounds, although watchful residents have interrupted attempted break-ins of the bike sheds.

SNAPSHOT: **SACRAMENTO'S METRO SQUARE**

Another development in Sacramento offers evidence that smart growth can, indeed, produce environmental benefits when compared to conventional sprawling developments. Metro Square comprises 46 single-family, detached homes built in 1998. It was so attractive to the home-buying market that it completely sold out on the first day its houses were offered. The development's "smart" features include its location one mile from Sacramento's city center, its compact lots situated around common green space, and its conventional grid-pattern streets.

A recent NRDC study found that, compared with two conventional suburban developments with the same number of single-family homes, Metro Square consumes only roughly one-quarter as much land. And, in contrast to the suburban developments, no agricultural land was converted in its construction. The study also discovered that, despite its use of alleys and wide sidewalks, Metro Square contains less paved surface per household and per capita than the conventional developments, reducing surface water runoff. Its more compact lots also reduce the need for pesticides and fertilizers, as well as water for irrigation during Sacramento's dry summers.

Unlike the conventional developments, Metro Square has many neighborhood amenities within walking distance, including a convenience store, a supermarket, a school, a park, and public transit service. It also features connected streets, bicycle network markings, crosswalks and other traffic controls at intersections, traffic-calming measures, and shade trees along its sidewalks, all of which make it more inviting to pedestrians and bicyclists than conventional developments.

While the study's analysis of residents' travel behavior was not sufficiently detailed to reach firm conclusions, the preliminary evidence suggests that the location and features of Metro Square may well make a difference in reducing driving and attendant motor vehicle pollution. Survey results indicate that Metro Square residents may be more than four times as likely as residents in conventional Sacramento developments to accomplish daily tasks by walking and may take only half as many driving trips, driving a total of between only 50 and 60 percent as many miles. This translates into fuel and energy saved as well as fewer emissions of greenhouse gases and unhealthy air pollutants.[14]

In the years preceding Southside Park's construction, a strong neighborhood association had made great gains in driving crime out. Now, with several active members from Southside Park joining them, the neighborhood group continues improving safety on the streets. Southside Park residents who came from "nicer" parts of the city or from the suburbs say they feel secure in their new neighborhood. "This area feels completely safe to me. I walk to work and run a lot of my errands on foot," says Susan Scott. One of her neighbors, Laurisa Elhai, made an unusual point: "You are not necessarily safer in a neighborhood with a better reputation." Her house had been repeatedly burglarized in her previous, more upscale, neighborhood, but she has had no trouble at Southside Park Cohousing.

MARKET-RATE PRICES
Apartments:
One bedroom: $88,000
Two bedroom: $134,000
Townhouses:
Two bedroom: $122,000
Three bedroom:$140,000
Four bedroom plus den: $150–160,000

The safe communal atmosphere has helped Southside Park children thrive. With 28 children from 2 to 17 years old living in Southside Park Cohousing full- or part-time, young people always find friends around. "When our children were smaller, it seemed like there was a slumber party at least once a week. Now there are always a bunch of kids hanging out on our front porch," recalls Susan Scott, who is a mother of three teenagers.

Besides the front porches of Southside Park residences, the new youth center provides another place for kids to gather. As of this writing, the popular recreational facility is temporarily located in a building near the neighborhood swimming pool. Partly as a result of years of lobbying by the neighborhood association, the city has finally budgeted the money for a brand new building with ongoing staff support.

The youth center is not only a great asset for children, but also a symbol of Southside Park Cohousing's positive role in the neighborhood. Cohousing residents worked hard along with other neighborhood activists to get the center built. Not surprisingly, the neighborhood residents, who were once resentful of the newcomers, now gladly accept them as part of the mix.

Free from the Daily Commute at Last

Mark and Theresa Tavianini used to live in Fontana, a typical bedroom community in southern California. Mark would get up at 5:15 each morning to drive to Los Angeles—a grueling 40 miles often choked with bumper-to-bumper traffic even at that early hour. Theresa commuted every day in the other direction, driving their second car, until their first son was born and she decided to stay home. It was a life that many other suburbanites share, but one they disliked. Mark, who works for the California Air Resources Board, also felt that his auto-dependent lifestyle went against his ideals for cleaner air. He looked into a transfer to Sacramento, where he could live closer to work. There, the Tavianini family found out about Southside Park Cohousing, and—after temporarily renting a house in an inner suburb—moved in as soon as it was built. Their second son was born shortly after the move.

Mark now bikes to work. Theresa still drives, but only five miles. She usually drops off the children at their schools, which are a mere six blocks from home (the boys, four and ten, are too young to walk alone). The family sold one of their cars. "I love the sense of closeness here," says Mark. "Nowadays, I rarely get beyond the six-mile radius of our home. I can just walk out of my house and easily get to where I need to be—shops, restaurants, the movies. And, of course, I don't have the drudgery of the commute every day. I now have quality time for the family and for myself." He pauses. "I got my life back when I moved here."

SUISUN CITY REDEVELOPMENT
SUISUN CITY, CALIFORNIA

In September 1999, the *San Francisco Chronicle* featured an article about Suisun City, a small city of roughly 27,000 residents, located some 45 miles northeast of San Francisco. The article had this to say about the town's recent past:

SMALL CITY MAKES A COMEBACK BY REDEVELOPING ITS CORE

> Just over 10 years ago, the town of Suisun City was in big trouble. Its downtown was near death, its waterfront was a mess, one of its neighborhoods was the drug capital of Solano County. Its city government was broke, and City Hall was situated in a large trailer. "It was the only city hall in California that was registered with the Department of Motor Vehicles," said James Spering, then and now mayor of the town. "Suisun City had every kind of problem," he said. "Social, economic, every stage of blight."[15]

Indeed, a previous *Chronicle* comparison of all 98 cities and towns in the Bay Area had rated Suisun City dead last. The comparison considered school test scores, housing prices, crime rates and other quality-of-life indicators.

But today, Suisun City has a new face—a new waterfront, a refurbished Main Street, new jobs, and a renewed identity. Suisun City's dramatic comeback demonstrates that smart-growth principles create not only livable but also economically viable places. And it shows that a declining community can take charge of its future and successfully undertake a major redevelopment effort.

Suisun City's waterfront promenade.

A Bedroom Community

The Patwin Indians once hunted and fished on the edges of the vast Suisun (pronounced suh-SOON; it means "west wind") Marsh, perhaps the largest saltwater wetland on the West Coast. With the California Gold

Rush came eastern settlers, who founded Suisun City in 1848 at the head of the winding Suisun Slough, 12 miles from the deep water. The slough made Suisun a bustling river port, and a shopping district and a cluster of Victorian houses grew along Main Street and in Old Town near the water. The community was an important enough commercial center for the transcontinental railroad to be routed through it in 1869, bringing more activity and wealth.

Almost a hundred years later, Suisun City was bypassed by highway I-80, and thus by new economic development. As in other parts of the country, the newer chain stores located along the highway. Whatever new tax revenues were generated went to the more fortunately located neighboring municipality, Fairfield.

By the 1980s, Suisun had lost its former glory. Its once lively Main Street was lined with boarded-up buildings and a few struggling businesses. The waterfront area bore the scars of an oil refinery operation and many years of neglect. Poorly maintained warehouses, leaking oil-storage tanks, and deteriorating docks dotted the shores of the small silted-up bay. There was no public access to the forgotten waterfront. People were afraid to go there anyway, because the nearby Crescent neighborhood was so drug- and crime-infested that over half of all police calls in the city were to this four-block area.

Nevertheless, the town's population tripled from 1970 to 1980. Commuters to the East Bay and San Francisco (45 miles) and Sacramento (30 miles) found Suisun's affordable home prices attractive. Vast, pastel-colored subdivisions were built as far away from the decaying town center as possible. Most newcomers worked, shopped, and pursued leisure activities outside of Suisun City. Suisun was losing its identity as a historic town and was instead becoming a suburban bedroom community.

A New City Hall Offers Confidence in Waterfront

In 1986, Suisun elected a new mayor, James Spering, a graphic designer turned reluctant politician, made redevelopment of Suisun City his highest priority. He believed that only major public investment would help Suisun, and that this investment should be targeted at the historic downtown and waterfront area.

The first major public investment of the Spering administration was building a new City Hall. In 1989, a $3.5 million glass-domed structure was erected on the derelict waterfront, in the vicinity of the crime-ridden Crescent neighborhood. "People thought I was nuts," recalled Spering in a *USA Today* interview, "but the city had to show confidence in the waterfront. We had to show what it could be, not what it was."[16]

Also in 1989, a citizen committee assembled to create a redevelopment plan for Suisun City. The committee brought together residents, business people, elected officials, planning staff, and architects to identify opportunities and roadblocks. After a long series of intensive discussions, they created a comprehensive blueprint. The so-called Downtown Specific Plan was adopted in 1991.

In the same period, the municipal redevelopment agency expanded its institutional capacity. In 1988, an experienced redevelopment specialist, Camran Nojoomi, became the agency's head. The following year, the local government consolidated the Planning and Housing Departments under the redevelopment agency's direction. Most important, the city raised significant redevelopment funds through a bold financing mechanism.

It was clear that redevelopment of Suisun City's decaying core would be expensive. Unfortunately, Suisun City could not realistically hope for major private sector investment or large amounts of state or federal money. The city had to find a way to raise its own funds for its ambitious redevelopment plan.

Declaring all of Suisun City a redevelopment Tax Increment Financing (TIF) zone provided the solution. This meant that all future increases in revenue, not only those directly linked to downtown development, would go toward paying off redevelopment bonds ($58 million dollars initially, with $10 million dollars added later). Essentially, the city decided to put *all* its financial growth toward redevelopment efforts, because it realized that redevelopment was the key to restarting its economic engine.

A Waterfront City Once Again

In the last decade, thanks to Suisun City's redevelopment efforts, the waterfront has become worthy of its handsome new City Hall. At the city's urging, the oil refinery/storage operation moved away from the waterfront and cleaned up its contaminated site. Improvements were made not only on the shore, but also to the slough itself. The City had the silted-up channel open by 1993, providing deep-water access. The extracted soils were used to create new wetlands on nearby Pierce Island, which had been used for sewage disposal in the sixties.

Thanks to the opening of the channel and 150 newly constructed, state-of-the-art berthing slips, the marina is now in heavy use. Furthermore, the cleaned-up waterfront is enlivened by a variety of new uses. A 5,000-foot waterfront promenade connects the entire waterfront to a popular Town Plaza, which features a raised stage area and a sloped lawn graced by eight towering palms. There are over twenty festivals and events scheduled annually, attracting as many as 150,000 spectators.

Also near the waterfront are a growing number of live/work units. Most famous among them is Babs Delta Diner. Its owner, Babs Curless, serves home-style cooking in the restaurant downstairs, and has her living quarters—with commanding water views—upstairs. When she rises at 3AM to start baking biscuits, she is especially grateful that she does not need to commute to work. Soon the waterfront will include more live/work units, a hotel, a professional office building, and a pedestrian-friendly development of single-family homes.

PRINCIPALS

Developer: Suisun City Redevelopment Agency
Design: ROMA Design Group
Public sector: Mayor and City Manager, City of Suisun City

The revitalization of the waterfront has also helped nearby Main Street, where over a dozen businesses have participated in the city's Facade Improvement Program, which provides matching funds for storefront renovations. Historic buildings are getting facelifts in other parts of Old Town as well, and some are being converted to new uses: a historic bank building is now home to a dance studio, and an old grocery store has been turned into a 170-seat community theater. The theater has enlivened the downtown with performances on almost every weekend, featuring professional and college acting, as well as children's plays.

To reclaim Suisun's role as a transit hub, the previously run-down rail depot at the head of Main Street was renovated and transformed into a facility also serving Greyhound, other local long-distance buses, and vanpools. Several new train routes were added, including Amtrak's Capitol Corridor commuter service, providing access to Sacramento and the Bay Area. Every day, 14 passenger trains stop at the Suisun City station, reopening a chapter from Suisun's past as a thriving railroad city.

Where the crime-ridden Crescent's dilapidated housing once stood, a new neighborhood with a new name and identity has taken shape. Victorian Harbor is today a community of 94 new, single-family houses on small lots that feature Victorian design and front porches. Garages are in the back, accessible from alleys. The tree-lined streets are narrower than in typical new developments to slow traffic, while the pedestrian-friendly sidewalks are wider. This all adds up to a walkable, pleasant neighborhood with a strong sense of community and character, and it sharply distinguishes Victorian Harbor from the automobile-dependent, monotonous subdivisions built in the 1970s and '80s at the town's edge.

While Victorian Harbor is market-rate housing, lower-income households can find housing options within the former Crescent neighborhood. Five single-family homes are set aside for moderate-income residents; a city-managed apartment complex of 52 units serves low-income tenants; and a HUD-subsidized complex, which was left in place, is now managed by a nonprofit corporation, providing a safe and comfortable home for still more low-income families.

Let Suisun be Suisun

It is to Suisun's particular credit that its redevelopment had a decidedly local flavor. The traditional focal points of the town—its waterfront and downtown area—provide the focal points of the revitalization. Instead of targeting large chain stores, the redevelopment effort focused on small local businesses, such as Babs Delta Diner.

Although Suisun's spectacular rebirth required substantial public funding—raised mostly from the local municipal bonds made possible through tax increment financing—the city joined with the private sector to get the job done. Much credit for the innovative redevelopment plan and design goes to the San Francisco-based ROMA Urban Design Group, while local designers and developers played major roles at the individual project level. In helping the private sector to do its job, the city was discerning in its choice of developers and did not settle for anything short of design excellence. Suisun also used state and county grants to help in the effort. For example, redevelopment of the train depot was only made possible with a half-million-dollar state grant.

Suisun City has stayed in charge of its own destiny throughout the process. Instead of sacrificing its identity for economic progress, it achieved success on its own terms. Significantly, the redevelopment effort strengthened Suisun City's identity as a small, thriving community. Camran Nojoomi, the executive director of the city's redevelopment agency, summed up the philosophy of the redevelopment effort: "We decided to let Suisun be Suisun."[17]

WESTMINSTER PLACE
ST. LOUIS, MISSOURI

A neighborhood formerly known as "the Stroll" for its heavy prostitution and drug trading did not seem to be a likely candidate for revitalization. But Westminster Place, a mixed-income housing development of 400 units in St. Louis, Missouri, succeeded in attracting a rich mix of residents to this troubled urban area. The secret of its success? Unorthodox design appealing to suburban sensibilities; redevelopment at a critical mass; the development of a shopping center next door; a healthy mix of incomes; and a convenient urban location close to job centers and cultural amenities.

FAMILY-ORIENTED HOUSING AND SHOPPING IN THE INNER CITY

Suburban Look, Urban Conveniences

The houses in this community are brand new. Some are free-standing single family homes with three bedrooms, two-and-a-half baths, a two-car garage, a deck and a full basement. Others have the look of a suburban mansion on the outside, but are in fact divided into four apartments on the inside. They symbolize Westminster Place's creative design solutions, which aim to appeal to suburban sensibilities while also fulfilling urban functions. The development offers a verdant look and a quiet feel, but without the inefficient low densities of sprawling suburban design. It speaks of middle-class security and values, but half the units are subsidized so that low-income households can afford them. It offers easy automobile access, but is within walking distance of shopping and several job centers. The grass and the shrubs could very well be in suburban St. Charles County, but in fact they are smack in the middle of St. Louis.

A pleasant walk in Westminster Place.

MCCORMACK BARON

Westminster Place is home to an unusual diversity of races, income levels, ages, and family arrangements, yet still maintains a strong sense of community. This is not by accident: half of its units were sold or rented at regular market rates, but the other half—indistinguishable from the market-rate units—has been set aside for low-income residents. There is a waiting list for these subsidized units, and tenants are carefully screened.

Most of the units are for rent, but the development does include 41 homes that were sold and are now privately owned. There is also a 96-unit facility for the elderly, comprising both subsidized and market-rate apartments. For frail seniors, this facility offers an alternative to living in a nursing home; their apartments are private, but meals, home health services, and transportation are provided for those who need them.

The 90 acres where Westminster Place stands today looked very different during the 1970s and early 1980s. In fact, the entire corridor between St. Louis's Midtown area and the Central West End was suffering from widespread disinvestment, blight, and abandonment. Many buildings had been demolished; others had been damaged by fire or slowly scavenged for salable building materials. Liquor stores and pawnshops occupied the few remaining streetfronts. Crime and drugs were plentiful. The intersection of Washington and Olive Streets, one of the city's infamous havens for prostitution, became known as the Stroll.

SMART-GROWTH FEATURES

▶ Mixed-income housing and racial diversity
▶ Many housing options: apartments, single-family houses, and units for seniors
▶ Major shopping center built within walking distance
▶ Revitalization of blighted neighborhood
▶ Urban housing that is attractive for families

Public-Private Partnership

A successful public-private partnership changed all that. In the early 1980s, Mayor Vincent C. Schoemehl Jr. and Richard Baron, a local developer who specialized in mixed-income housing, began to discuss plans for the neighborhood's redevelopment. While the site itself was badly blighted, the surrounding area promised positive influences. Just to the south lay St. Louis University's large campus. To the east, St. Louis's performing arts corridor, including the historic Fox Theater, was only blocks away. On the west, private streets and lovely historic homes bordered the area. The central business district was only three miles away, and two large medical centers—one to the southeast, the other to the southwest—were both within a half-mile, promising interest from professionals in housing options at the site.

In 1983, the city designated the 90-acre site a redevelopment area, and Baron's company, McCormack, Baron & Associates began construction of 163 residential units, the first phase of Westminster Place. In 1985, McCormack Baron and Leo Eisenberg jointly developed Lindell Market Place, a 145,000-square-foot shopping center, providing residents with a very convenient shopping venue. The center features a National supermarket, a Blockbuster video store, and a number of smaller, minority-owned businesses, including neighborhood services and restaurants.

Residential construction proceeded through the 1980s and '90s, including the construction of the homes for sale. The American Cancer Society relocated its headquarters to a Westminster Place building completed in 1995. By 1995, a new church and a new magnet high school were built on a block adjacent to the supermarket. Construction of the complex for the elderly came last, beginning in 1998.

The city provided significant financial support for the project. A number of state and federal funds were also used, including Community Development Block Grant Funds, tax exempt bonds, mortgage insurance, and low-income tax credits.

Market Success

Westminster Place has been popular in the marketplace. By the late 1990s, occupancy rates were as high as 98 percent. Aggressive marketing and inviting people to the site were critical to attracting residents in the beginning. As the development grew and the neighborhood stabilized, Westminster Place maintained its popularity. Significantly, not only the usual "urban pioneers" have chosen to make their homes here, but professionals and families have as well. As the laughter of children fills the air on summer weekends and people walk their dogs across the verdant landscape, it is hard to imagine that less than two decades ago this was a dreary and dangerous place.

3

Smart Suburbs

Are we satisfying our deepest yearnings for the good life with Edge City? Or are we poisoning everything across which we sprawl?

—Joel Garreau, *Edge City*

The questions Garreau poses are important, because it is likely that the bulk of American development over the next few decades will, as in the last few, take place outside of central cities: in suburbs and on the expanding suburban fringe. Put another way, urban redevelopment and rural preservation by themselves won't be enough. To solve sprawl, we must also solve suburbs.

Over the past five decades, many American citizens and businesses have been moving to and among suburbs in search of affordable land and housing, good schools and public services, a convenient lifestyle, and peace and quiet, among other attributes. Those of us who have located in these areas have found some of these qualities, but too often we have also found a lot that we didn't bargain for, including mind-numbing traffic congestion, ugly strip development, isolated workplaces, rising tax rates, and a lack of character and interesting places among our homes, shops, and workplaces. As a result, suburbanites today are often among the strongest advocates of smart growth. A nationwide poll undertaken by the Pew Center found that suburban residents were much more likely than city dwellers to classify sprawl as a critical problem in their communities.

Fortunately, some of the most creative and successful alternatives to sprawl are, in fact, being developed in the suburbs. The examples in this chapter illustrate a number of different settings and approaches that are helping American suburbs solve sprawl to the benefit of the environment, the economy, and our social interactions.

Creating Town Centers

Some of our examples respond to one of the most frequent complaints about sprawl: that, in a seemingly disconnected jumble of separated housing subdivisions, office parks, and shopping strips, it lacks a sense of place. People feel that sprawl has few of the important elements of their lives within walking distance or even an easy drive, and has little that establishes any shared sense of community among residents or workers. Some of this is even mandated by a now-outdated patchwork of zoning restrictions that are piecemeal rather than cohesive and that prevent homes, workplaces, and shops from locating conveniently near each other.

Addison Circle north of Dallas and Reston Town Center in northern Virginia, near Washington, D.C., are two smart new places that take a different approach: the creation of vibrant, walkable "town centers" within suburbs that reduce the need for driving while mixing shops, offices, civic functions, entertainment, and residential units. Mashpee Commons, on Cape Cod in Massachusetts, and Orenco Station, outside Portland, Oregon, also contain some features of town centers, although on a smaller scale.

Reclaimed Shopping Centers and New Main Streets

Eastgate Town Center in Chattanooga, Tennessee, presents a variation on the town center theme: a walkable, mixed-use development incorporating offices, shops, and recreation and educational facilities on the site of what was formerly a failing shopping mall. Such conversions are important because, while suburban shopping centers are far from a dying breed, many older malls have lost their commercial appeal and are failing, leaving large parking lots, abandoned buildings, and wasted infrastructure behind. The Crossings is a large residential development of nearly 400 units built on the site of an abandoned shopping mall in Mountain View, California. Bethesda Row, in suburban Maryland just outside Washington, D.C., offers a highly successful example of a related genre: a "Main Street" approach to creating a lively commercial strip on a once-declining street.

Developments with Transportation Choices

One of the most challenging tasks in making suburbs smarter is making them less automobile-dependent. Bethesda Row, mentioned above, is also an example of a new commercial strip that provides real transportation choices, with homes and offices within easy walking distance, a major bus and rail transit station only a couple of blocks away, and a popular bicycle and hiking trail just across the street and leading all the way to downtown Washington. Two additional examples, Orenco Station and The Crossings, are transit-oriented developments where local municipalities worked with private developers specifically to create walkable, convenient communities adjacent to commuter train stations. Village Green is also within easy walking distance of good transit service.

Affordable Housing

Some of our examples seek to remedy a different but common suburban problem: a lack of affordable housing, especially near workplaces. This forces starter households and others to flee even farther to the metropolitan fringe in search of homes they can afford to purchase or rent; it reduces community diversity; and it exacerbates the harmful effects of driving by lengthening commuting distances. Solving sprawl requires that we build reasonably priced suburban housing—not just premium housing and commercial space—in smart ways. Among our examples, Village Green in Los Angeles consists entirely of affordable units, as does Third Street Cottages near Seattle and Everett, Washington. The residential portion of the Burnham Building in New York also comprises affordable units.

Reinvestment in Inner-Ring Suburbs and Older Communities

As the examples of dying shopping malls illustrate, it is important to recognize that suburbs are not all alike: they span a wide continuum, from old to new, poor to rich, declining to growing. A common challenge is that, while some older, inner-ring suburbs enjoy prosperity and stability, others are now struggling with issues once thought of as exclusively urban, such as poverty, neglected housing, and overall decline and disinvestment.

The First Suburbs Consortium in the Cleveland metropolitan area provides an inspiring example of inter-jurisdictional cooperation among various inner-ring suburbs that are solving these problems. Eastgate Town Center is another example of revitalization in a declining older suburb, and the redeveloped Burnham Building, although not located in a classic inner suburb, is an excellent model of smart renovation of a declining property in an older town that is now part of metropolitan New York City. Third Street Cottages offers an example of a small-scale, smart-growth development in a town now feeling development pressure from nearby Seattle and Everett, Washington.

Suburban smart-growth solutions frequently differ in scale, style, and type from those of their city counterparts and, indeed, there is much variation from suburb to suburb and project to project. This chapter highlights a few real-life examples of these solutions.

ADDISON CIRCLE

ADDISON, TEXAS

Addison Circle offers an oasis of excitement in an area that has long epitomized some of the worst aspects of disorganized, chaotic suburban sprawl. Demonstrating the viability of a more coherent, place-based approach, the new development features a rich mix of homes, shops, and offices, with attractive buildings close to pedestrian-friendly sidewalks, small com-

AN EDGE CITY REDEFINED WITH A WALKABLE, COMPACT CENTER

munity parks, and an elegant boulevard. In addition, the ground floors of some residential buildings are enlivened by cafes, restaurants, and convenient neighborhood services such as dry cleaners and fitness clubs. Hallmarks of Addison Circle include attention to architectural detail, an active street life, and city-style conveniences. It has become what Addison, Texas, had painfully lacked—a place with identity, character, and heart.

A Fading Edge City Finds New Center

Before Addison Circle was built, the Town of Addison, 12 miles north of Dallas, was a typical edge city. Development was heavily skewed toward the commercial side: in 1996 some 160,000 people worked there, but only 10,000 called themselves Addison residents. The town had successful restaurants, hotels, and office developments along the

Dallas North Tollway but as new development spread farther and farther north, some of its businesses followed. The town realized that it needed to create a better sense of place in order to set itself apart from other sprawling suburbs, to keep its businesses, and to attract more residents. To do this, the town formulated an ambitious long-range vision for a vibrant town

A pocket park in Addison Circle.

center where new residents and neighborhood business could congregate. But first, an appropriate site had to be found.

The land that became Addison Circle was an open field that hosted the town's annual Oktoberfest but was known for little else. Surrounded by sprawl, the field no longer had much value for wildlife or other conservation purposes. However, at 80 acres, the site was large enough for developing an ambitious smart-growth project. And its location was ideal, within walking distance of workplaces, shops, and entertainment. It also was close to Addison's existing conference and arts centers, and adjacent to a regional bus hub and proposed light-rail line. And it was helpful that the property had a single landowner, Gaylord Properties that was willing to form a long-term development partnership with the town of Addison.

The town recruited a developer, Columbus Realty (now Post Properties), and reached out to the Gaylord family. The three parties negotiated a 15-year plan for the site. They agreed that any adjustments in the plan had to go through a public input process, called Vision 2020.

The public sector's contributions to the development included financial and zoning support. It gave $4.5 million in infrastructure improvements, and tentatively committed another $4.5 million for additional improvements, contingent on the development's progress. The town also agreed to fund the upkeep of streets and parks and invested in a new conference center, a theater, and public art. Most important, it reformed regulations and zoning that would have stood in the way of creating a walkable, compact, mixed-use neighborhood in a suburban setting.

Columbus Realty/Post Properties brought a wealth of experience to the project and helped educate town officials and citizens about the planning and design elements of successful multipurpose developments. Today, Addison Circle is in many ways a showcase example of smart growth: it is built on an infill site, close to public transportation; its

TIMELINE

1995: Public/private partnership is formed; 15-year plan is written   **1996**: Construction begins   **1997**: Phase I is completed   **2000**: Phase II is completed, bringing the development to 1,100 apartments, 110,000 square feet of shops, 300,000 square feet of office space.   **2001**: Phase III and beyond includes thousands of residences, 300,000 square feet of additional retail space, and over 1 million square feet of office space

Interaction among neighbors and participation in local institutions helps foster what we call "community," a sense of belonging to a place. The design—and frequent chaos—of sprawl, can discourage these activities. First, low residential densities and the lack of neighborhood stores force people to leave their communities for basic shopping errands, social visits, and work. Since automobile travel is often the only means of achieving this, suburban residents tend to interact with their neighbors mainly through their windshields—a decidedly anti-social form of human interaction. The relative absence of pedestrian activity is a particular threat to community cohesion, because walking is conducive to chance encounters and the maintenance of informal relationships within communities.

In addition, many edge cities and other new, outer suburbs exhibit a striking lack of political coherence, along with relatively few civic and cultural institutions to provide any sort of unifying force. Cul-de-sac street design also prevents individual developments from connecting with each other and, in some cases, walls and gates are erected for the very purpose of isolating developments from the outside world.

Time spent in traffic also takes it toll. According to a recent market research survey, Americans now spend roughly one out of eight waking hours in their cars. The additional time spent driving eats directly into leisure and professional time. In addition, as every soccer parent knows only too well, a shortage of time only compounds the challenge of balancing work and personal responsibilities, particularly for working mothers. The inevitable result is stress, fatigue, and less time with family. Moreover, the lack of real transportation choices in outer suburbia has a particularly isolating impact on those who cannot drive, including the elderly, people with disabilities, low-income individuals, and youths.

Smart growth helps restore a sense of community by building more compact neighborhoods that are walkable, with sidewalks and safe street crossings as well as home and shop entrances close enough to the street to be convenient and inviting. Smart-growth developments also contain or are built near a diversity of institutions and neighborhood amenities, such as convenience stores, shops, restaurants, movie theaters, post offices, schools, and other meeting places. By having these locations within walking distance, especially when developments also have good public transit options, residents enjoy more free time because they need not drive so much.

combination of over a thousand apartments and townhomes makes full use of the site, yet on a human scale, with four-story buildings and attractive community parks and public squares; it places shops and services within walking distance of residents, and employs wide sidewalks, arcades, and a pleasant streetscape to entice pedestrians.

A Success on Many Fronts

As of July 2000, 95 percent of the completed 1,070 apartments at Addison Circle were occupied, and more than 80 percent of the shopping space—planned for about 40 proprietors—had been leased. The office buildings were also proving successful, ultimately renting out in record time in a competitive market.

PRINCIPALS

Developer: Post Properties, Inc. (formerly Columbus Realty) **Design:** RTKL Associates, Inc., Dallas Public sector: Town of Addison **Other:** Gaylord Properties (landowner)

People are attracted to Addison Circle for its quality of life. "I know my neighbors here, and I never knew anyone where I lived before," said Celia Newman, a small-business owner and Addison Circle resident, to the *Dallas Morning News.* She is also happy that her 25-year-old son lives in her building.[1]

All told, Addison Circle is a striking alternative to the sprawling development that characterizes so much of the Sun Belt. Because it uses land efficiently, it saves open space in the Dallas metropolitan area. Because it accommodates people on foot and puts residents near jobs and shops, it saves automobile trips and prevents air pollution while enhancing social contact. It also brings a well-planned architectural character to the chaotic and disconnected mishmash that dominates edge cities. As John Williams, the chief executive officer and chairman of Post Properties, put it: "Visiting Addison Circle is like stepping into an environment apart from everything else in the Southwest."[2]

BETHESDA ROW
BETHESDA, MARYLAND

Only a few years ago, the five-block area that is today called Bethesda Row was an unremarkable suburban thoroughfare for automobiles, with outdated and underused shops, low-rise office buildings, and surface parking lots. Today, the development is one of

A SUBURBAN MAIN STREET

the most popular parts of Bethesda, Maryland, an upscale inner suburb of Washington, D.C. It is also a successful, smart suburban alternative to a sprawling shopping strip.

View from a Balcony

It all started in 1994, thanks to a strategically oriented balcony, where a group of employees of Federal Realty Investment Trust's Bethesda office were taking a break. They had been searching for a model project to pioneer the real estate investment company's new strategy of acquiring large multiblock sites and turning them into vibrant shopping and entertainment districts. "Why not here?" someone asked, pointing to an area visible from the balcony. The area had a strong potential customer base, and it already contained a public garage. It was also accessible by Metro, the regional subway system.

Best of all, the five blocks in question had a single owner who was willing to work with Federal Realty. This saved the company the usual trouble associated with acquiring land for larger infill projects: the sometimes painfully slow acquisition of land, parcel by parcel. In addition, county officials were already promoting development around Metro transit stations and, in fact, had designated the area where Federal planned Bethesda Row for Main Street-style shopping. This was obviously

Good food and conversation on Bethesda Row.

very helpful in gaining overall county support for the Bethesda Row concept.

However, the county planners' vision did not always match Federal Realty's idea of what would create an attractive and economically viable shopping street. The two sides struggled with disagreements over spending priorities, such as whether to invest in brick sidewalks and ornamented streetlights (the city's plan) or in large trees and high-quality storefronts and awnings (Federal Realty's idea). Eventually, county leaders stepped in to iron out the differences between the developer and their agency's staff.

SMART-GROWTH FEATURES
- ► Infill development
- ► Mixed uses
- ► Pedestrian-friendly design
- ► Accessible by transit
- ► Accessible by bicycle
- ► A suburban "Main Street"

Besides the challenge of reconciling competing visions, Federal Realty ran into a now-familiar problem faced by communities attempting to implement smart-growth strategies: outmoded, inflexible zoning codes and regulations that stand in the way of innovative ideas. For example, the project's main architect, Richard Heapes, had a vision of an open outdoor cafe area in front of the restaurants and shops. He wanted to pull the outdoor seating areas a few feet away from their respective cafes and restaurants, so that strollers walking alongside shopping windows would not be interrupted. But city regulations required that any outdoor seating be attached to the building and cordoned off from the street. Eventually, the regulation was relaxed, to the satisfaction of merchants who now have a steady supply of passersby, and to the enjoyment of visitors who can see window displays on one side of their path and cafe patrons dining and conversing on the other.

A Smart Vision Realized

Federal Realty's planners envisioned a public gathering place on the corner, in front of what is now a Barnes and Noble bookstore, featuring movable chairs and a fountain symbolic of the angel Bethesda. But the company's property managers initially opposed using fountain stones that might be picked up and thrown, and leaving the chairs without securing them with chains. The planners prevailed. "In the last four years, no one has ever touched the stones, and only a few chairs

PRINCIPALS
Developer: Federal Realty Investment Trust
Design: Street Works
Public sector: Montgomery County Planning Board
Other: Bethesda Urban Partnership

have disappeared," points out Nathan Fishkin of Federal Realty. "When people value a place, they protect it."

Because the fountain and chairs are right across the street from the Capital Crescent Trail, a converted railroad line that is now a popular bicycle and hiking route running from Bethesda to downtown Washington, it is not uncommon to see tired cyclists sitting on the chairs and sipping drinks, with their bicycles safe in the provided racks.

In fact, one of the development's best features is that, unlike conventional shopping malls and strips, its employees, restaurant patrons, and shoppers have a choice of how they get there: they can choose to drive and park at a public garage within the development, of course, but they can also bicycle, walk from nearby

> **PROJECT DATA**
>
> On 8.1 acres:
> **Existing:**
> Total: 388,200 sq.ft.
> Retail: 225,900 sq.ft.
> Office: 160,600 sq.ft.
> **Planned:**
> Retail: 20,000 sq.ft.
> Theater: 30,000 sq.ft.

housing and offices, take Metrorail trains to the Bethesda station only two blocks away, or ride a bus to any of the several stops within easy walking distance.

A Sense of Place

Today, with the bookstore, trendy shops, and restaurants, Bethesda Row's brick sidewalks bustle even in the winter with strolling visitors from the neighborhood and beyond; when the weather warms up, they relax outdoors on the public benches and movable chairs around the fountain, or in street-side cafes. A large art film house, now under construction, will introduce a new entertainment option. Offices are located above the shops, restaurants, and theater, placing workers within easy reach of the Row's shops and services.

The buildings in Bethesda Row are generally two to four stories. Designed by four different architectural firms, they feature diverse building materials and architecture. In a highly unusual move for a new development, the design of the storefronts was left to the tenants. The result is an interesting mixture, including some eye-catching, unique elements. For example, Sansar, an independent store selling contemporary American arts, features a grid of glass panels with patterns of etchings on its exterior. Next door, the awning of Aveda, a national cosmetics chain, juts out in a bold triangle in contrasting yellow and gray.

These two stores exemplify the diversity of merchants found in Bethesda Row. Interestingly, local and regional tenants outnumber nationals. Diversity benefits visitors—on a day trip, they can do every-thing they could do at a large mall, and more, including grocery shopping, dropping off dry cleaning, getting a haircut, shopping for clothes, art, and cosmetics, and stopping for coffee and bagels. Visitors can also have a night out at one of the several restaurants, then peruse books at Barnes and Noble. They can easily walk from one place to another, enjoying chance encounters and window-shop-ping. No wonder the streets of Bethesda Row are always busy.

"It actually surprised us that people come here to go to a restaurant or to shop from as far away as Fairfax," comments Richard Heapes, refer-ring to another metropolitan Washington suburb across the Potomac River in Virginia. "While this is a great retail district, it should not be so special. Every neighborhood should have a pedestrian-friendly shopping and entertainment area—including the suburbs."

BURNHAM BUILDING
IRVINGTON, NEW YORK

Irvington, New York is an incorporated village of 6,000 people in the lower Hudson River Valley, north of New York City, near the better-known towns of Scarsdale and White Plains. Although it was long an independent town, Irvington today functions, like its neighboring towns

AN INDUSTRIAL BUILDING BECOMES A LIBRARY AND AFFORDABLE HOUSING

in Westchester County, as a suburb of New York City, to which it has been linked by train—first steam, then electric—for more than 150 years. For today's commuters, Grand Central Station is a convenient 37-minute express train ride away.

The Irvington train station is located at the bottom of the principal commercial strip, Main Street, on the once-industrial waterfront. Across from the station stands the landmark Burnham Building, now 120 years old. Like the station, the building has both historic and modern-day significance for the community: what was once a distinguished manufacturing plant is now—after a period of abandonment and threatened demolition—an innovative combination of public library on the ground floor and affordable apartments above.

From Factory to Library

The Burnham Building once produced greenhouses and conserva-

The library in the Burnham Building.

tories for America's most wealthy patrons, including structures now at the New York Botanical Garden. The Lord & Burnham Company, which used the facility for light manufacturing and offices for over a century, also manufactured cast iron boilers. In 1988, however, the company closed the location, leaving the Victorian-style wood frame and masonry structure vacant.

FREDERICK CHARLES

For almost half a decade, people getting off the train in Irvington were greeted by the sorry sight of the abandoned building across the street.

But Irvington needed a new, expanded library, and the Irvington Library Board of Trustees, in charge of choosing the new location, had the wisdom to see the potential of the Burnham Building. Of course, extensive renovations

and retrofitting would be needed to convert the abandoned industrial building's ground floor into a modern library. In late 1992, the citizens of Irvington voted yes on a bond referendum raising money for the project.

A few months after the referendum passed, Irvington bought the 30,000-square-foot building. Since only the ground floor was needed for the library, the three upper floors remained available for additional development. After considering plans for offices and shops, the Village Board (Irvington's legislative body) decided instead to accept a developer's proposal to convert the remaining space into 22 of Irvington's first affordable rental apartments. Before this proposal, Irvington essentially had no affordable housing, although plans had been made for creating some.

A Multi-Sector Partnership

In 1995, the Burnham Building redevelopment project stalled, because the housing developer was unable to raise enough funds for the project. The village then turned to the Katonah, New York-based Affordable Housing Development Corporation (AHDC) to serve as developer. In turn, AHDC helped to bring Greyston Foundation, a nonprofit organization, on board for ownership and management of the affordable units. The Supporters of Village Library, a group of private donors, also joined the partnership.

This broad partnership, involving the public sector, a private development company, a nonprofit organization, and a group of local donors, worked very well. With AHDC's leadership, the team succeeded in identifying a variety of funding sources for the project, including local, state, and federal government grants and loans, private financing, and charitable donations. Most notable among the donations was $1.2 million from the Supporters of Village Library.

In April of 1998, construction commenced. In spite of the difficulties of working on an old, historically significant structure, the housing units were completed by September 1999, and the library opened its doors to the public in January 2000.

A Model of Smart-Growth

The Burnham Building redevelopment is a model smart-growth project in many respects. First, it demonstrates the benefits of historic preservation. The distinctive industrial building provides a link to Irvington's past and strengthens the village's identity.

Second, the redevelopment has contributed to downtown revitalization. By anchoring Main Street with a civic function, the Burnham Building enriches and strengthens the heart of Irvington. It has also sparked interest in the revitalization of the waterfront, including the creation of a 13-acre waterfront park.

Other significant smart-growth features are the project's pedestrian-friendly nature and easy transit access. Burnham Building residents can walk to local attractions, or take the train to Manhattan or other destinations along the route. Train users can also conveniently stop at the library without getting into their cars.

In addition, the Burnham Building makes the community's housing stock more diverse and puts people who otherwise could not afford to live in Irvington close to their work and families. But that is not all: on top of its other attributes, this is an outstanding model of energy efficiency and other green building features.

Adaptive reuse of historic structures almost always translates into significant savings of both energy and material resources when compared with construction of new buildings. Such resource-intensive activities as site clearing and foundation construction, among others, can be avoided, and new wood and mineral resources need not be used for structural features that are already in place. And, in this case, the renovation paid particular attention to environmental issues. For example, the builders made recycling a major focus. Historically significant doors and windows were identified before construction, then disassembled, refurbished, and reused. Construction wastes were also separated and recycled.

PRINCIPALS

Developer: Affordable Housing Development Corporation
Design: Stephen Tilly
Public sector: Village of Irvington
Other: Greyston Foundation (nonprofit partner, manager of affordable units); Irvington Public Library; Guiteau Foundation (nonprofit partner and large donor)

Reinvestment in existing structures is often made challenging by building codes designed only for new construction and adopted when an automobile-dependent culture was taken for granted. Requirements for everything from stairway and window dimensions to street setbacks and parking spaces, although well intentioned, can stand in the way of smart-growth adaptation of existing streetscapes. Maryland Governor Glendening has remarked that it would have been illegal to build the historic and popular state capital city of Annapolis under the building codes in effect in his state in the 1990s.

Fortunately, states are beginning to amend their codes to facilitate smart growth. In 1997, for example, the State of New Jersey adopted an innovative urban code to encourage the renovation of decaying buildings. Within a year, rehabilitation investment statewide rose by 8 percent. In the cities of Newark, Jersey City and Trenton, spending increased by 60 percent, 83 percent and 40 percent, respectively. Gains in Newark totaled $41 million. Maryland enacted a similar law in April 2000.[3]

Further energy savings were achieved by retrofitting the building with the most up-to-date energy-saving devices. For example, the building uses triple-glazed windows and cellulose fiber insulation. A community room for residents, with solar-powered heating and cooling, was built on the roof. More traditional techniques, such as strategically placing shade trees, were also used to help achieve significant overall reductions in energy use. Other environmentally significant features include the use of non-evaporative paints and building materials that cause less air pollution and pose fewer health risks than traditional paints and materials, and the replacement of formerly paved surfaces with gardens that reduce water runoff into the Hudson River and enhance the community aesthetically.

Making the Burnham Building Affordable

The Burnham Building brings affordable housing to Irvington for the first time in the village's long history. In the second half of the nineteenth century and in the first half of the twentieth, Irvington was best known for its opulent estates. Even though some of these estates were broken up and replaced by single-family housing and some condominiums and garden apartments in the decades after World War II, real estate prices overall have remained high. Right now, the average house in Irvington sells for around $450,000. Apartment rents start at $1,000 to $1,200. Clearly, these prices are beyond the reach of most middle- to lower-income people.

Not surprisingly, demand was very high when the Burnham Building offered Irvington's first affordable housing opportunity. Six of the 22 units were set aside for holders of federal rent-subsidy vouchers. Tenants for these six units were chosen from a waiting list of 50 applicants. The other apartments were designated for lower-income village residents, relatives of residents, and people who worked in Irvington. More than 150 applications were received for the remaining 16 units. To qualify for an apartment in 1999, a single person's income could not exceed $16,800; a family of four's could not exceed $47,940.

The selected residents are of varied ages. Some are young people under age 30, who previously had been forced to live with their parents because of high housing prices in the area. Middle-aged residents and families who hold low- and moderate-income jobs in Irvington are also part of the mix.

And as many as a third of the Burnham Building's residents are seniors on fixed incomes. For many, this is an opportunity to have a decent place to live while remaining close to family. For example, Virginia Fiorito, a retired secretary, moved from another town into a one-bedroom apartment to be close to her son and grandson, who live in Irvington. "I had been looking for years for affordable housing," she said in an interview with *The Rivertowns Enterprise.* "It was like a dream come true."[4]

THE CROSSINGS
MOUNTAIN VIEW, CALIFORNIA

As we saw in the preceding chapter on smart growth in cities, one of the most environmentally promising alternatives to conventional sprawl is transit-oriented development: compact, walkable, diverse neighborhoods around public transit stations. Pedestrian-friendly design, proximity to shops and offices, **A TRANSIT-ORIENTED NEIGHBORHOOD ON RECLAIMED LAND** and good transit access can reduce the need to drive. Efficient use of land also reduces the pressure for conversion of open space and environmentally valuable land elsewhere in the region.

The Crossings, built around a new commuter train station, is a model of transit-oriented development. Indeed, The Crossings is an especially laudable example, because it contains a variety of housing types, was built on the site of a failed, automobile-dependent shopping center, and made extensive use of materials recycled from the old facility.

From an Abandoned Mall to Transit-Oriented Development

The suburban city of Mountain View, California is located in the booming Silicon Valley area between San Jose and San Francisco. By the 1990s, the region had been experiencing a large influx of people and housing for decades, and many residents had begun to clamor for limits on the density of development. But 200,000 additional people

Different housing types in The Crossings.

were expected to move to the county in the next 15 years, and a low-density approach would inevitably have driven growth outward, in the form of sprawl, and destroyed open space. Instead, the city argued, the best way to accommodate the expected growth was to increase density in designated zones. In particular, the city emphasized the need to concentrate housing

at transit facilities, like the Caltrain commuter rail station planned for the neighborhood where The Crossings is now located, in order to maximize the rail system's potential to help alleviate growth in traffic.

The shopping mall that originally occupied the site failed in 1991. In the wake of the failure, the city of Mountain View proposed a zoning change from commercial to residential use and held public hearings to plan for the 18-acre site.

After rejecting an initial design proposal, city officials requested

that the developer, TPG Development, hire a noted transit-oriented planner, Peter Calthorpe, to revise the master plan and design The Crossings. Less than five months later, a Calthorpe plan, incorporating a combination of small-lot, single-family houses, townhouses, row houses, and apartment units in a space-efficient layout was approved, and construction began.

Green Construction, Market Success

As much as possible, the developer recycled materials from the demolished shopping mall on the site. For example, waste materials were incorporated into concrete slabs and porches of new buildings, crushed into gravel, or used as landscaping materials for the new development's pocket parks. In this case, recycling was not just the right thing to do environmentally; it also proved to be less expensive than shipping out the waste products.

To help with paying off the $20 million debt TPG had inherited from the failed mall, the single-family homes (the most profitable unit type) were developed and sold first. Next came town- and row houses, then condominiums, with a 200-car parking garage for Caltrain users underneath. Altogether, over 300 homes were built. The finishing touch was the 2,000 square feet of retail space incorporated into the area near the train station, to serve the shopping needs of commuters and residents.

The developer paid special attention to design details that foster community. An interconnected pattern of tree-lined streets, neighborhood parks, and pedestrian paths knits the neighborhood together. The *New York Times* described The Crossings as a "village of pastel-colored homes, pocket parks, sidewalks, and gazebos," pointing out some of the pleasant, attractive features of the residential area.[5] Families find The Crossings's playgrounds, small parks, and neighborliness especially appealing, and children are a common sight. Many residents walk to work at the several large offices nearby. For their neighbors who commute, the train station, with its frequent service to Silicon Valley and San Francisco, is a significant asset.

> **PROJECT DATA**
> On 18 acres:
> ▶ 97 single-family houses
> ▶ 30 townhouses
> ▶ 99 row houses
> ▶ 171 apartments and 2000 sq.ft. retail

Shopping is also within easy walking distance of all the residences. A large Safeway supermarket, which predates The Crossings, is right behind the townhouses, while Sears and other shops are just across the train tracks.

The Caltrain station, the neighborhood's main entry point, opened about a year behind schedule, in April 1999. But, now that the trains have arrived, The Crossings is functioning as it was envisioned by the Calthorpe plan—as a transit-oriented, livable community.

A Market for Compact Development

The design of The Crossings has yielded a relatively high average density for the development of 22 units per acre. But this density does not create a sense of crowding or restriction. As resident Bob Michel told the *San Francisco Chronicle:* "It's not at all confining, since you can walk to everything."[6] Others note that the parks, wide sidewalks, lush landscaping, and pleasant streets create a feeling of spaciousness.

In fact, despite claims that consumers dislike density, the market has clearly embraced all the housing choices at The Crossings.

T I M E L I N E

1991: Old mall closes **1994:** Calthorpe begins plans **1995:** Single-family homes **1996:** Townhouses **1997:** Shops, row houses **1998:** Condos built **1999:** Caltrain opens station

In his 1985 book *The Malling of America,* W. S. Kowinski described enclosed suburban shopping malls as "the culmination of all the American dreams, both decent and demented, the model of the post-war paradise." Indeed, in the 1970s and 1980s, these shoppers' "par-adises" were being built at such a pace that it seemed inevitable they would permanently replace downtown department stores, Main Street retailing, and other traditional shopping venues all over the country. In many places, they have.

However, success has come at a price, as fierce competition among malls has now created an oversupply of shopping space. In just 13 years, between 1986 and 1999, the amount of retail space for every American grew by a third. The United States currently has nine times more retail space per capita than it did in 1960. In 1999, there were 20 square feet of shopping mall space for every man, woman, and child in the United States, and 13 percent of that space was vacant or abandoned.

In addition, a number of still-functioning malls are failing or vulnera-ble. A recent study of regional malls by PriceWaterhouseCoopers finds that 6.7 percent of them are failing. In the next five years, the number of failing malls will increase by as much as 12 percent, the same study conservatively predicts. Other experts predict that as much as 15 to 20 percent of shopping malls will close in the coming years, given their current oversupply and the advent of electronic shopping.

The first to go are often the older malls. The average age of the typi-cal failing mall in the PriceWaterhouseCoopers study was 32 years. The steady decline in these malls often reflects the overall decline of the older, first-ring suburbs where many are located. Fortunately, the Crossings and Eastgate Town Center demonstrate that smart-growth opportunities can lie in redevelopment of old, failed shopping malls. The revitalization or adaptive reuse of old malls can act as a powerful catalyst for revitalization of the larger community.

According to the Center for Livable Communities, its homes were the fastest selling in the region. This demand has made home ownership a profitable investment for Crossings residents. In only a few years, resale values were about $100,000 over the original prices. As the *San Francisco Chronicle* comments: "What it offers is an option—another way that people can live in what once were the suburbs. And the more options we have in the Bay Area, the better off all of us will be."[7]

EASTGATE TOWN CENTER
CHATTANOOGA, TENNESSEE

The rise and fall of Eastgate Mall is typical of first-generation shopping malls. Eastgate was built on farmland eight miles east of downtown Chattanooga in the early 1960s, making it one of the very first suburban-style, enclosed shopping malls in the country. Eastgate's neighborhood, Brainerd, is within Chattanooga's city limits but, having been developed in recent decades, it has a suburban feel. An exciting novelty, the mall quickly became popular. In the process, unfortunately, the mall also drained commerce from downtown Chattanooga and contributed to the inner city's economic decline.

AGING MALL GETS NEW START AS TOWN CENTER

In the late 1970s and early 1980s, Eastgate Mall itself began to decline. New highways diverted traffic from the boulevard it fronted, and the mall building started showing its age. Some tenant stores began to leave, and the flow of shoppers declined. Then, in 1986, the bigger, flashier Hamilton Place Mall opened six miles farther east, sealing Eastgate Mall's fate. JC Penney, one of the two anchor stores at Eastgate, moved to Hamilton, and many others followed. By the early 1990s, more than 70 percent of Eastgate was vacant. The large swath of its concrete parking lot, once full of cars, stood almost empty; the mall itself, once teeming with shoppers, was eerily quiet even on weekends. Eastgate Mall became a thing of the past—a dreary, forgotten site.

From Call Center To Town Center

Eastgate was saved by the convergence of public initiative and private investment. On the public side, a new mayor, Jon Kinsey, ran on the platform of revitalizing the Brainerd neighborhood. Shortly after his election, he commissioned the Regional Planning Agency to study options for reviving the failed mall site. As a result of its study of successful models nation-

SMART-GROWTH FEATURES

▶ Reuse of aging, economically failing, shopping mall
▶ Mix of offices, shops, restaurants, entertainment, and civic functions
▶ Attractive public spaces
▶ Pedestrian-friendly design, bus access
▶ Revitalization of neighborhood
▶ Intensive public input

wide, the agency recommended that the mall be redeveloped as a mixture of offices, shops, civic organizations, and perhaps even residences.

Independent of this public effort, Norman Harrower, a California businessman, had also become interested in the mall. Harrower came to Chattanooga in 1997 to look for potential locations for a large corporate telephoning and customer service center. As an outsider, he brought a fresh perspective. Seeing beyond the failed mall, he found the site's plentiful parking, good access from a busy seven-lane boulevard, and affordability attractive. At his recommendation, his local partner, Gerry Chauvin, assembled a group of investors to create Eastgate Enterprises. The group bought Eastgate Mall in the summer of 1997 with plans to redevelop it as a corporate "call center."

Even though the new owners could have built the call center by right, and thus were not obliged to negotiate with the city over permits, they were willing to listen to the city planners' ideas for the site. In the end, the investors embraced the city's goal of bringing mixed uses to Eastgate Mall. The new owners even agreed to elicit public input for the plan and design of the redevelopment.

Vision Emerges from Public Meetings

The developers hosted a series of public meetings to shape the design of the Eastgate redevelopment, with the help of a professional team including designers, traffic engineers, and retail specialists. These charettes, where participants got a chance to see their ideas transformed into site maps and drawings, involved as many as 250 people. "The meetings had an emotional overtone, because of the many memories Eastgate Mall evoked," recalls Rick Wood, an urban planner who represented the city. "Some people recalled seeing their first movie, or experiencing their first kiss in the mall. Once people realized that Eastgate Mall could get a new lease on life, they enthusiastically

Top: Eastgate before redevelopment. Center: The near future at Eastgate Town Center. Bottom: The long-term vision for Eastgate.

PRINCIPALS

Developer: Eastgate
Enterprises LLC
Design: Dover, Kohl, and
Partners
Public sector:
Chattanooga/Hamilton
County Planning Agency;
Office of the Mayor, City
of Chattanooga

contributed their ideas." The local television news followed the proceedings.

A town center concept emerged from these meetings. The windowless, big-box buildings of Eastgate Mall would be turned inside out, with street-facing windows for ground floor shops, and large windows for offices that would be housed above. The development would be renamed Eastgate Town Center and would feature a mix of offices, shops, and restaurants, as well as educational, recreational, and civic organizations. At its heart, a green public square would provide refuge and a chance to socialize for office workers, shoppers, and other visitors. A series of tree-lined pedestrian walkways would encourage people to stroll throughout the development.

A Diverse Mix of Tenants

As of this writing, two and a half years after the public meetings took place, Eastgate Town Center has succeeded in securing a strong office base and diverse recreational and educational resources. Thousands of jobs have been created at the center, largely because Eastgate Enterprises has succeeded in recruiting three insurance giants as well as Convergys (formerly AT&T Solutions), with approximately 850 employees in its call center. (This much of the original plan survived.)

The mall was not demolished, but it underwent extensive retrofitting to accommodate the new uses and a modern-day workforce. BlueCross/BlueShield occupies the former JC Penney store, which underwent a $5.5 million facelift. The call center occupies space formerly used by other department and clothing stores.

The first services to come to the new Eastgate were those catering to the office workers: dry cleaners, banks, an optometrist, cafes, and restaurants. More recently, they have been supplemented with several clothing and other shops for the broader public, such as successful Gap and Nine West outlet stores. A couple of family restaurants, including a steak house, have also opened.

In addition to the offices, shops, and services, recreational and educational facilities help create activity around the clock at Eastgate Town Center. In particular, Chattanooga's YMCA has moved to Eastgate, offering a plethora of fitness options, as well as child care services. Another popular recreational amenity is a seasonal, open-air ice-skating rink. Perhaps more than any other feature, the rink has attracted residents from Chattanooga and surrounding suburbs to rediscover Eastgate as a regional attraction.

In addition, Chattanooga State Technical Community College has located a satellite campus at Eastgate, offering a number of courses, including some that are specially targeted to different groups of Town Center employees. For example, a legal assistance class was developed to meet special needs identified by BlueCross. The 25 employees who took the class in the winter of 2000 enjoyed the convenience of strolling over to school after work.

Fewer Automobile Trips

While many employees still drive to Eastgate Town Center, they can run their various errands on foot during the day and after work. They do not need to make a detour in the morning to drop off their children at daycare, to have a cup of coffee and a muffin, or to stop at the dry cleaner. They can walk to lunch; and they can shop or work out in the evening—all within Eastgate. Eventually, planners hope that more employees will choose to use mass transportation to commute to work. There is already good bus access to Eastgate Town Center.

The high-profile Eastgate redevelopment has also boosted the image of the aging and previously stagnant Brainerd neighborhood. The $30 million investment has brought valuable new resources and opportunities into the neighborhood, serving old-time residents and attracting newcomers. Indeed, other businesses along Brainerd Boulevard, a typical sprawling commercial strip, have looked at the success of the reconfigured Eastgate site and embarked on redevelopment plans themselves.

During the last years of the failing mall, even Brainerd-area residents who could have walked to Eastgate chose instead to drive the seven miles to Hamilton Place Mall. That is changing today. "I used to come here all the time, and then Hamilton

EASTGATE TENANTS

Office:
► BlueCross/ Blue Shield
► Cigna
► Merastar
► Convergys

Shops and restaurants include:
► Gap outlet
► Nine West outlet
► Applebee's
► Schlotzsky's Deli
► Christopher's Steak House

Recreation:
► YMCA
► Ice Rink

Education:
► Chattanooga State Technical Community College

Services:
► Champion Cleaners
► Union Planters Bank
► Health House of Chattanooga
► Police precinct

Today, Chattanooga is celebrated as a model sustainable community whose citizens work together in creative ways to solve environmental, economic, and social problems. But it wasn't always so: in 1969, Chattanooga was the city with the worst air pollution in the United States and faced additional serious problems including layoffs, a deteriorating city infrastructure, racial tensions, and social division. Recognizing these challenges, a few visionary community leaders got together and created Chattanooga Venture, a nonprofit organization with the mission of focusing the community's attention on improving their city.

In 1984, Chattanooga Venture brought together more than 1,700 citizens in a city-planning project called Vision 2000. Over the course of many meetings, diverse groups brainstormed, debated, and organized their concerns and ideas into a set of 40 goals for the city to achieve by 2000. The goals covered a wide spectrum from creating a distribution and transportation center, to strengthening the downtown area, to solving pollution problems, to strengthening the city's day-care system and creating after- and before-school programs.

Today, many of the original goals of Vision 2000 have been achieved. The city now meets federal air quality standards and maintains the largest fleet of free, nonpolluting electric buses in the United States. In addition, the Tennessee River Gorge Trust now protects 25,000 acres of ecologically, geologically, and archaeologically rich land, and the Greenways Planning Project is creating a network of protected areas of open space and parkways through eight nearby counties. Issues of economic and community welfare are being addressed by the Chattanooga Neighborhood Enterprise, a nonprofit organization devoted to developing, financing, renovating, and managing affordable housing for low- to moderate-income citizens. Jobs 2000, a project of a regional economic development agency, is working on strategies to eliminate inequities in employment, with a focus on minority empowerment. Other groups are working on redeveloping the city's riverfront, with a riverside park and a nationally renowned aquarium already open.

Altogether, Vision 2000 has been credited with bringing Chattanooga more than 200 projects and programs, creating nearly 1400 permanent jobs and over 7,000 temporary construction jobs, and attracting a total financial investment of nearly $800 million to the area. Spurred by this success, the community updated its plans in 2000 (ReVision 2000), again using an extensive public process.

As a result, Chattanooga is now recognized as a "living laboratory" for sustainable development projects. Indeed, Vision 2000 has published a handbook for communities interested in undertaking a similar process, and has advised nearly a hundred cities from around the world in the areas of sustainable economic development and urban design, citizen involvement, minority empowerment, and alternative transportation options. The Chattanooga Neighborhood Enterprise and the Tennessee Aquarium, for example, have already inspired similar institutions in other communities.[8]

Place was built, and when the stores started to move out there, that's where I went. But there is just something special about [Eastgate]. It brings back a lot of nice memories and I've thoroughly enjoyed coming back to it. Since I live out in this area, it's also so much more convenient," says Mary Wylie, who now spends her evenings walking around Eastgate Town Center.

FIRST SUBURBS CONSORTIUM
METROPOLITAN CLEVELAND, OHIO

Smart growth is not just about buildings, streets, and landscapes. It is about people, of course, and sometimes it is also about creating new civic institutions to deal with the problem of an inadequate local political structure. One of the most challenging of these is the lack of forums for cooperation among the

INNER-RING SUBURBS PURSUING COMMON GOALS

many individual jurisdictions that make up our metropolitan areas. When these jurisdictions plan and develop independently rather than cooperatively, one community's gain frequently comes at another's expense.

Challenges Facing Older Suburbs

The consequences of failing to cooperate are felt acutely in the inner-ring suburbs of America's older industrial cities, such as Cleveland. In many of these places (including Cleveland), metropolitan areas have continued to sprawl outward in recent years, even while overall populations have declined. At the same time that substantial new investments have been made to develop new subdivisions and the infrastructure to support them, existing communities have suffered from a

SMART-GROWTH FEATURES
▶ Voluntary regional cooperation among previously competitive municipalities
▶ Reinvestment in existing communities
▶ Support for housing renovation, brownfields redevelopment, and strengthening older shopping districts

lack of funds. The resulting decline of the older communities tends to create still more sprawl which, in a vicious circle, leads to still more disinvestment in the inner-ring suburbs.

Ken Montlack, vice-mayor of Cleveland Heights and a founding member of the First Suburbs Consortium, gets upset when he hears someone talk about "the suburbs" in general terms. He knows all too well the difference between older, inner-ring suburbs, with their aging housing stock and flat or diminishing tax base, and the newer, outer-ring suburbs where the moving trucks—as well as investment dollars—are heading these days.

Indeed, a number of inner-ring suburbs around the country are experiencing problems that have traditionally been considered urban

- Urban
- Inner ring suburbs
- Outer ring suburbs

ills. According to PriceWaterhouseCoopers' and Lend Lease's *Emerging Trends in Real Estate 2000,* as many as 400 suburban jurisdictions now meet the federal government's criteria for distress: population decline exceeding five percent and poverty rates over 20 percent. And these distressed suburbs seem to have benefited less from the recent economic good times than cities. Unemployment is shrinking more slowly in the suburbs than in central cities, for example.

In fact, older suburbs can find themselves at a disadvantage compared with both central cities and newer suburbs. On the one hand, inner-ring suburbs are less likely to have cities' cultural and entertainment attractions, which can lure people and businesses back; they qualify for fewer federal and state assistance programs; and, in general, they have less political clout to fight for resources. On the other hand, while new suburbs receive large amounts of state and federal money for new roads, schools, sewers, and other infrastructure, there are no similar funds going toward reinvestment in existing structures in older suburbs. "We are invisible," says Ken Montlack.

Collaboration, Not Competition

The First Suburbs Consortium is a new institution that aims not only to bring more visibility to the Cleveland area's inner-ring suburbs, but also to channel more resources their way. Originally an informal cooperative body of representatives of a few municipalities, in 1997 it was institutionalized as a Council of Governments that includes twelve municipalities.

Typically, a region's municipalities compete—sometimes fiercely—for new businesses, people, and other resources. It is proof of the forward-looking leadership in greater Cleveland that these competing tensions were put to rest for the overall good. The decision to cooperate, rather than compete, is especially impressive if we consider that, superficially, some member municipalities might appear to have less incentive to do so than others.

For example, three First Suburbs communities that abut Cleveland-Shaker Heights and Cleveland Heights on the east and Lakewood on the west—are relatively well to do. They boast well-maintained historic architecture,

Cleveland and surrounding consortium suburbs.

Cuyahoga County

healthy cultural institutions, and proximity to thriving employment and education centers. They are historically diverse communities, established in the 1920s as streetcar and trolley suburbs of the central city.

In contrast, other First Suburbs members, such as Garfield, Euclid, and Maple Heights were built after World War II. Parts of these communities are industrial; the bungalow-style housing was built for blue-collar workers. As the housing stock becomes dated and shows signs of age, and as newer suburbs lure people further out, these communities are hurting more than their prosperous neighbors.

In spite of these differences, the leaders of the inner-ring suburbs realized that they shared many important concerns. While their housing stocks might have been of different ages and values, they all needed repair and reinvestment. Streets, sewers, and other infrastructure were also showing their age. And even the more affluent communities were witnessing population declines and a diminishing of income levels. "We are not anti-development," explains Keith Benjamin, the staff administrator at First Suburbs Consortium. "We believe that people and businesses should be able to go and live and/or work wherever they choose. But not at the cost of the older, mature communities. We need to start thinking more equitably and look at ourselves, not individually, but as part of a larger region. It's all about equity."

"HELP" for Home Renovations

All First Suburbs members fall within Cuyahoga County, which makes it easier to institute some cooperative programs without going through the state government. One county-level program that was designed with the input of the Consortium and that especially benefits inner-suburban residents is the Home Enhancement Loan Program, or HELP. In it, the county invests in certificates of deposit at participating banks at below-market rates, in exchange for the banks providing home improvement loans for qualifying residents at below-market rates. In effect, the county buys the loans down by three percentage points, for example, from 9 percent to 6 percent. The program helps people stay in the county's vulnerable communities, while providing incentives for long-term improvements to the communities' housing stock.

People qualify to participate in the program if they live in one of the 32 target communities (12 of which are the consortium members), if they are creditworthy at the subsidized rate, and if their houses are worth no more than $250,000. Participants are free to shop around for the best loan terms among the different participating banks. The lending institutions are solely responsible for the lending criteria and loan default risk.

HELP, which is run out of County Treasurer James Rokakis's office, has proven to be very popular. In just 16 months, the total amount of closed loans stands at almost $30 million. More important, there are both market and survey indications that a number of people decided to undertake home improvements only because of the availability of the lower interest rate, and that many people would have moved if not for the improvements to their homes.

Under another countywide program that was influenced by the First Suburbs Consortium, $40,000,000 has been made available to help local communities pay for cleanup and redevelopment of contaminated properties. In 2000, its first year, only inner-ring suburbs were eligible. The program should be a tremendous help to industrial towns like Euclid.

Updating Shopping Districts and Attracting Developers

While the county initiated and runs HELP, another planning initiative, Main Street Connections, was financed and coordinated solely by the First Suburbs Consortium. In particular, the consortium retained a retail development consultant to study two shopping districts in each member municipality. A yearlong research process yielded a set of recommendations for each district, such as zoning and coding changes, financial packaging options, streetscape and marketing improvements, and changes to the tenant mix. This advice is especially useful for smaller member municipalities, which have a shortage of planning and financial experts on staff.

The Consortium also plans a development council, which will provide "one-stop shopping" for developers interested in investing in any First Suburbs municipality. The council will keep a database of available properties and provide expert development advice. Consortium members are now raising money to create this new resource.

FIRST SUBURBS CONSORTIUM

Bedford
Cleveland Heights
Euclid
Garfield Heights
Lakewood
Maple Heights
Shaker Heights
South Euclid
University Heights
Warrensville Heights

None of these initiatives is a panacea, and Cleveland's inner suburbs will continue to face challenges as they seek to rehabilitate their communities. But, as with all smart-growth solutions, every step forward helps. And when steps are put together, they can add up to a whole new way of developing. Cleveland's First Suburbs are now thinking collectively, and they are on the right path.

It is remarkable how far the First Suburbs Consortium has come since 1997, the year it was officially launched. When asked about the key to success, both Montlack and his colleague Keith Benjamin, a Cleveland Heights development officer and First Suburbs Consortium staff administrator, point to visionary leadership and to a spirit of genuine cooperation.

As Benjamin puts it: "These elected officials—very different people, from very different communities—have come together, and are making history. They share a strong commitment to break down barriers that separate their communities, and to make a difference jointly. It's a truly remarkable example of cooperation."

MASHPEE COMMONS
MASHPEE, MASSACHUSETTS

The New Seasbury Shopping Center, located in the small western Cape Cod town of Mashpee, Massachusetts, was originally built in the mid-1960s. Located at the intersection of Routes 28 and 151, the development was typical of the time: it featured single-story buildings surrounded by an expansive parking lot. It was **FROM STRIP MALL TO NEW ENGLAND VILLAGE CENTER** frequented by shoppers from Mashpee and two nearby towns, as well as by Cape Cod's growing seasonal population of tourists and second-home owners.

By the 1980s, the shopping center had become dated and was ripe for renovation and expansion. But Buff Chace, son of the original developer, didn't choose just to expand the old mall. Instead, he and his partner, Douglas Storrs, formed a new business venture and undertook a more ambitious project: to transform the old shopping center into a walkable, mixed-use village center built in traditional New England style. Unlike many New England small towns, Mashpee had never had an old-fashioned village core. That was the void that Mashpee Commons would fill.

Chace and Storrs were ahead of their time, creating a model smart-growth development before anyone had even heard of the terms "smart growth," "new urbanism," or "traditional neighborhood design."

Shopping and living in Mashpee.

The New England Village Core Model

Chace and Storrs began to research traditional New England small-town layout and architecture in 1984 with a tour of nearby villages and some distant towns. They catalogued indigenous physical characteristics, such as granite curbs, tree-lined streets, and small-scale brick and clapboard buildings. They even measured the widths of streets and sidewalks. While Mashpee Commons was not simply going to imitate a nineteenth-century look, the developers learned a great deal about what made these older communities walkable, neighborly, and charming.

Chace and Storrs realized that, in order to create a vibrant village center of sufficient size, Mashpee Commons would have to be larger than the old shopping center. They acquired additional land on both sides of Routes 28 and 151, for a total of 255 acres.

The development process started in 1986 with a series of local public meetings about the new village center's design. The developers submitted a master plan for the site to town officials and, after extensive negotiations over the design, the town granted a permit for development of the three-block commercial core of Mashpee Commons. That same year, construction began.

The first phase was completed by 1988, and additional construction has continued. In just two years, striking transformations had taken place. Even though the old shopping center was not dismantled, it became hard to recognize. Buildings were transformed by renovations to storefronts and rooflines. Alterations were also made in the massing and scale of buildings. The largest original tenant, a department store, was bought out by the development company and its space divided among smaller shops. Most significantly, the area behind the shopping center was given a completely new look, with New England-style two-story buildings lining the streets and shielding the parking lot from view.

Many of the new two-story buildings feature small offices above shops, in the fashion of a historic downtown. The second-floor space of one of the newest buildings is all residential units. There was an 80-person waiting list for its 13 units when they opened, proving the existence of strong pent-up demand for the conveniences of in-town living even in a traditionally low-density, resort area. A housing complex for elderly people, containing 24 units, also adds to the vitality and diversity of the town center.

Support for Mom and Pop Stores

The bustling street life at Mashpee Commons is living proof of the new town center's popularity. In fact, the shops at the Commons generate among the highest sales per square foot on the entire, heavily commercialized Cape Cod peninsula. In other words, they are outperforming strip, shopping, and outlet malls. In fact, even when comparisons are made on a national scale (using Urban Land Institute surveys), Mashpee Commons generally falls in the top 10 percent of community shopping centers in rent value and sales per square foot.

In particular, as Mashpee Commons has grown and become better known, sales revenues have gone up. Since 1992, individual store revenues have consistently risen annually. By the late 1990s, some of the shops were among the best performing in their chains. For example, Puritan Clothing, a well-established regional chain, says its Mashpee store has the highest sales per square foot of any of its stores. The Gap also reports that Mashpee Commons is one of its most profitable locations nationally.

While rising rents may ultimately favor national and regional tenants with deep pockets, the development company has made a conscious effort to keep mom-and-pop stores as part of the mix. Some of the most recently completed retail spaces are deliberately small, making them affordable. Value is placed on attracting unique, local tenants. Once at Mashpee Commons, local stores get ongoing advice and help from on-site support personnel from the development company.

SNAPSHOT: CONSERVATION AND WASTEWATER TREATMENT

The master plan of Mashpee Commons calls for 50 percent of its property to be set aside as open space. Some of this open space is inside the developed and to-be-developed areas—for example, in the form of small neighborhood parks—but there are also large tracts of land at the edges of the development that will be left undisturbed. These include environmentally sensitive areas; for example, land next to a river is reserved on the western side of Mashpee; land next to a pond is reserved on the eastern side. Fifty acres in the southern part are classified as primary conservation land. By not developing at all in these areas, the development company is able to transfer development rights (see Glossary) to the central parts of Mashpee Commons, and thus make these core areas more compact, convenient, and vibrant.

In addition to this protection of its environmentally sensitive buffer areas, the river's health is safeguarded by using a state-of-the-art wastewater treatment system. The buildup of nitrogen in waterways poses a serious problem on Cape Cod, because of the omnipresence of polluting septic systems. Mashpee's output will be less than one-seventh that of a standard septic system. In fact, the developers hope to connect the septic systems of surrounding buildings into their wastewater treatment system, and thus achieve an overall *reduction* of nitrogen pollution in the community.

The streets themselves are also different from the norm. In contrast to the wide expanse of asphalt typical of roads in new developments, Mashpee Commons's streets were designed not just for cars but also for pedestrians. To keep the streets small-scale and safe, there are only two traffic lanes on each, with on-street parallel parking; the sidewalks are wide, attractive, and tree-shaded. A traditional grid pattern provides easy traffic flow for both pedestrians and drivers.

Besides being easy and pleasant to get around on foot, Mashpee Commons also encourages walking by bringing many facets of life—and many typical destinations—into a compact area. In addition to the large variety of shops, offices, and restaurants, there are such services as banks, dry cleaners, a post office, a drug store, and a large supermarket. The local library, the fire and police departments, and a church are nearby, at the commercial center's western edge. They were built on land donated to the town of Mashpee by the development company. During the warmer seasons, a festival tent is set up at Mashpee Commons, hosting a full schedule of concerts, performances, and special events.

Mashpee Commons's compact, walkable design and central location reduce driving by allowing customers and residents to substitute trips on foot for errands that otherwise would require a car, and by shortening distances for those who do choose to drive. But the Commons also offers other transit options. Although the population and layout of Cape Cod do not support urban-style public transit such as light-rail, there are three bus stops in Mashpee Commons, with connections to other parts of Cape Cod. The developers hope that, as more communities on the peninsula embrace the village center concept, bus service will become more widely used. Mashpee Commons by itself has already contributed to some increase in regional bus ridership.

Village Housing

The new village center is clearly a success, embraced by locals and visitors alike, and performing well in the market. However, there is also a more ambitious vision in the works: the master plan for Mashpee Commons includes five neighborhoods in addition to the commercial core described above. This plan builds on Storrs's and Chace's original concept, which has been refined by the pioneering new-urbanist architects Andres Duany and Elizabeth Plater-Zyberk. Some of the planned neighborhoods, which were designed with the assistance of public input, would feature shops and offices similar to the ones in the commercial core, while others would be primarily or entirely residential.

PRINCIPALS

Developer: Mashpee Commons Limited Partnership
Design: Imai/Keller Inc.; Duany Plater-Zyberk and Company

Altogether, 380 homes are planned. Some of these will be apartments above shops like the ones built in the commercial core; others will be townhouses, and yet others single-family homes. In fact, one neighborhood will consist of all single-family housing on lots ranging from one-eighth to one-fifth of an acre.

It is important to note that, in evaluating whether a development is sufficiently compact to be labeled "smart growth," it is *average* density that counts: although the plan for Mashpee Commons contains some lots that approach conventional size, the development is smart because it contains a large variety of housing types, sizes, and lots at an overall average density much greater than that associated with sprawling developments.

The Mashpee Commons plan is also smart in a number of other ways. While each neighborhood will have its own set of characteristics, they will all feature pedestrian-friendly streets, a set of neighborhood parks and community gathering places, and traditional New England-style architecture. The neighborhoods and commercial core are interconnected and form a cohesive community where people live, work, shop, and play. Ten percent of the Commons' planned residential units will be kept affordable.

When Zoning Isn't Your Friend

So far, the neighborhood most similar to the commercial village center is the only one that has received regulatory approval. As of this writing, 83,300 square feet of shops and offices have been built in the North Market Street section, following the granting of a development permit in 1993.

The experience of the remaining neighborhoods is, unfortunately, all too typical of the frustrations and hurdles that can await planners, developers, and communities that try to fashion creative smart-growth solutions where outdated zoning and building codes still stand. As is the case with most suburban zoning codes in the United States, Mashpee's prohibits the mixing of commercial and residential areas, buildings that come up right to the sidewalk, narrow streets, and many other essential and "smart" features of the planned Mashpee Commons neighborhoods. In the case of the commercial core, a lengthy regulatory process was prevented by keeping the streets private and

Developments like Mashpee Commons and Bethesda Row are part of a growing movement to make suburban shopping and offices more hospitable to pedestrians and more oriented toward their communities than strip developments and large, enclosed shopping malls tend to be. Here are three more examples:

Mizner Park (Boca Raton, Florida)
A successful mixed-use development becomes an "instant downtown"
A centrally located but failing shopping center surrounded by parking lots in Boca Raton was transformed into a lively, mixed-use development with shops, housing, and offices flanking a grand, tree-lined public promenade. Designed by the same architects as Bethesda Row, Mizner Park's 40 businesses are not visible to cars on the adjacent main roads, but are oriented to the pedestrian plaza. It is conveniently located near the most densely developed residential area of the city, and the project itself houses about 480 residents. Mizner Park has become an "instant downtown" for Boca Raton and a popular gathering place throughout the day and evening.

Streets of Woodfield (Schaumburg, Illinois)
"Unmalling" a mall to create a Main Street environment in an edge city
A 700,000-square-foot, two-story, inward-facing mall has undergone conversion into an outward-facing streetscape of shops, restaurants, and entertainment venues creating a downtown atmosphere. An outdoor plaza features new facades, benches and gazebos, a valet parking area, trellis-covered cafes, boutique retailers, fountains, and gardens. Streets of Woodfield provides a much-needed central gathering place for employees and residents of Schaumburg, a booming, automobile-dependent edge city near Chicago known more for concrete than community.

Downtown Silver Spring (Silver Spring, Maryland)
A large-scale town center planned for an older suburb of Washington, D.C.
Although previous experiments to revitalize downtown Silver Spring have failed, a new public-private partnership holds great promise. Combining all the components of traditional downtowns, the development will include neighborhood shops, restaurants, the performing arts, a civic center, and downtown housing. The already-built first phase of the development includes a 70,000-square-foot Fresh Fields/Whole Foods Market and a Strosnider's Hardware Store, a Maryland business, complemented by a variety of smaller neighborhood stores. Later phases will bring Borders Books, a large movie-theater complex, a hotel, a large office building, and a 160-unit apartment complex, along with civic buildings and gathering places. The development plan is the product of an inclusive planning process that takes community needs into account. Cable-TV giant Discovery Communications recently announced that it will build its world headquarters in downtown Silver Spring, adding to the sense of optimism about the area's future.

therefore not subject to dimensional requirements that would apply to public streets. As a result, the area did not need to be rezoned from its existing commercial designation.

However, zoning changes were necessary to realize the rest of the Mashpee Commons master plan. For example, the mixed-use and residential areas use space much more efficiently than baseline zoning in Mashpee called for: a minimum of one acre per commercial property and two acres per home. The development company engaged Mashpee residents in an extensive public-education campaign about the advantages of a village center over sprawling development. After local officials recommended that the zoning changes be approved, a two-thirds majority vote was delivered at a town meeting to approve the zoning changes.

The local community has come to endorse the Mashpee Commons concept. However, given the overall size of the plan, regional and state permits are required in addition to the local zoning changes. These processes have also proved to be lengthy and difficult.

But, with luck, the rest of the Mashpee Commons dream won't stay on hold for much longer. Doug Storrs predicts that his company will receive all the necessary permits by the end of 2001. As soon as it has all the permits, it will embark on building the rest of the neighborhoods called for in the master plan. "I am absolutely convinced that this is the right plan for this part of Cape Cod or, for that matter, any community in New England," he says.

ORENCO STATION

HILLSBORO, OREGON

Although Oregon is well known for its progressive growth management policies, greater Portland is not immune to the problems that plague new, poorly planned suburbs elsewhere in the country, such as main arteries with soulless strip-mall development, isolated residential areas, and automobile dependence. People who live at the edges of Portland, like

A COMPACT COMMUNITY WITH DIVERSE HOUSING OPTIONS

those who live in most new suburbs elsewhere, must get in their cars to go to work, to drop off clothes at the dry cleaner, or to eat out. Those without access to a car or who cannot afford a single-family home are essentially excluded. Single people and empty-nesters who seek a different kind of lifestyle also find few choices that meet their needs.

On the other hand, Portland is doing something about it. While several metropolitan areas have recently been building new light-rail lines and expanding existing ones beyond their core cities, Portland has been the first to combine its extensive light-rail expansion into the

One of the main streets in Orenco Station.

suburbs with deliberate transit-oriented development around the stations. This coordination of transportation and land-use planning is a very promising trend. Not only are previously isolated communities being connected to downtown and to each other by light-rail, but the stations also serve as a focal point for creating walkable, vibrant, mixed-use pockets in suburbia. Orenco Station, in the Portland suburb of Hillsboro, is an outstanding example of such a development.

A Livable Neighborhood

Orenco Station is a new, 190-acre community, substantially but not yet fully built as of this writing. It is green, quiet, and safe, just like any desirable suburb. However, it is anything but a typical suburban development. First of all, it has a heart: a community shop-

PACTRUST

ping and gathering place. Within a five-minute walk, every Orenco Station resident can reach the town center to grab a coffee at Starbucks, shop for specialty wines, get a new prescription and eyeglasses, or enjoy delicious restaurant fare. Another notable feature of Orenco Station is the diversity of housing choices, including single-family homes, townhouses, loft apartments, and condominiums. One

choice that merits special mention is the development's live/work units, which transform the notion of the morning commute from a grueling drive to a walk down a few stairs to the first floor of one's own residence.

For those who work outside of the neighborhood, Orenco Station offers multiple commuting choices. Most prominently, the community is anchored by a light-rail stop, linking residents to the regional transit system. Free light-rail passes are provided to all newcomers for their first year, encouraging them to try transit. In fact, according to a 1999 neighborhood survey, more than one-fifth of households had at least one member taking light-rail regularly, and over one-half of residents were using it more often than they had thought they would. In addition, many residents choose to walk or bicycle to their nearby offices. And many of those who drive have only a short commute, since Orenco Station is situated within Portland's high-tech corridor and its many workplaces.

Turning Challenge into Opportunity

The parcel where Orenco Station stands today was originally slated for commercial and industrial development. In the early 1980s, Hillsboro began assembling land to lure high-tech companies to the area. One of the private development companies helping Hillsboro was Pacific Realty (PacTrust), which had acquired a number of the assembled parcels, including the future Orenco site.

Then, in the early 1990s, Portland's Westside light-rail line was approved, with a stop planned adjacent to the property. In order to receive funding for the light-rail, Hillsboro was required to rezone the area around the stop from the original commercial-only use to accommodate a compact, mixed-use development.

PacTrust faced a substantial challenge. It had not planned to build a mixed-use community on the parcel and, as a commercial development company, it had no expertise in such projects. Should it sue to keep the property zoned for commercial use? Should it get rid of the parcel?

Instead of fighting or giving up, PacTrust chose to embrace the challenge. Looking at its new situation with optimism, the company could sense opportunity. Also, the company's chief executive officer was himself a local resident, and he saw the value to the community of an innovative new development. The company initiated a series of meetings with Hillsboro planners, the Portland regional planning authority (Metro), and the regional public transit agency (Tri-Met) to work out planning guidelines. Once it was clear that the new development would have a strong residential component, PacTrust also joined with Costa Pacific Homes, an award-winning residential builder with local expertise.

Public-Private Partnership—Each Doing What It Does Best

As is often the case with smart-growth developments, a key to Orenco Station's success has been the public entities' willingness to give private developers flexibility in devising their own ways to meet public needs. "The public agencies did what they do best—setting worthy policy goals. We did what we, as a private company, do best—finding out what would sell in the market and delivering it in an innovate and cost effec-

Serenity and smart growth together in Orenco.

tive way," says Mark Mehany, project manager for PacTrust. "We actually became more ambitious than we would have been under more prescriptive guidelines, because we were in control of our risk management." For example, PacTrust experimented with narrow streets and houses sitting close to the sidewalks to encourage a walking environment. In spite of conventional wisdom among

As we build homes, workplaces, and shops, we must find or build a network of infrastructure to serve them. In addition to the driveways and utility lines that are needed on each building site, there are a number of categories that are typically furnished by the community at large, frequently at public cost. These include neighborhood costs such as streets, water distribution lines, sewer collector lines, and recreational facilities; community costs such as roads, water and sewer trunk lines, electricity lines, telephone lines, schools, emergency services (police, fire, and rescue), libraries, and parks; and regional costs such as regional roads, central water and sewer treatment, solid waste disposal, and central electricity and telephone facilities. Sprawl development costs more across all categories because it requires more infrastructure and more travel for service per unit.

With more compact, planned growth, on the other hand, the need for new infrastructure and services can be reduced, because growth can be directed to areas with existing service capacity, such as schools with additional classroom space. Where new infrastructure must be built, smart growth requires less of it to serve the same number of new units and also enables economies of scale for some services such as water and wastewater treatment.[9]

developers (also held by many public sector planners) that an automobile-oriented clientele prefers wide streets and that front yards are essential, the alternative features did well in the market.

In fact, market research pushed the developers not toward a more traditional suburban design, but rather toward bolder innovations. Early in the process, a survey of 1,500 local employees revealed important information about the housing interests and needs of potential residents. A majority of respondents who indicated an interest in living in a community like the still-evolving Orenco Station placed a high priority on walkable streets, neighborhood shopping and meeting places, commuting options, and a sense of community. Potential residents also expressed nostalgia for the "great old neighborhoods" of past eras. Many of the respondents were single, couples with no or few children, or empty nesters, all market segments poorly served by sprawling subdivisions.

The planners found innovative solutions to provide these amenities. For example, communal green spaces provide beautiful vistas and encourage encounters between neighbors. The compact design helps put more people within walking distance of the light-rail stop and the commercial portion of the development. Putting garages behind houses (they are accessible from alleys), another innovative design idea, not only strengthens the pedestrian environment, but also enhances the "great old neighborhood" feel of the community. Instead of driveways and garage doors, passersby are greeted with porches and varied design elements of English cottages and Craftsman bungalows.

Orenco Station is proof that traditional sprawling suburban development is not the only choice that sells well in the market. Not only have sales been high, but also the units command as much as a 25 percent premium over other suburban homes in the area, even though the latter have larger square footage and yards. This is especially impressive given that the original Orenco Station parcel had no natural amenities such as water, scenic views, or even large trees. Today, the large communal green space and the parks throughout the development provide attractive substitutes for the missing natural amenities.

Costa Pacific was so encouraged by the market success of Orenco Station that it has purchased a large parcel on the other side of the light-rail stop and is planning to develop it, too, according to smart-growth principles. Eventually, the catalyst of the original development—the transit stop—will be at the heart of an even larger extended community.

RESTON TOWN CENTER
RESTON, VIRGINIA

Reston Town Center is smack in the middle of sprawling, suburban northern Virginia in Fairfax County. Yet it has surprisingly urban features, such as high- and mid-rise offices with shops and restaurants at street level; movie screens only a short walk away; and an impressive hotel with a bustling, highly pub-

AN ISLAND OF SMART GROWTH IN A SEA OF SUBURBIA

lic lobby. Outside, the streets are busy with people shopping, chatting, and walking around. On nice days, office workers and visitors eat their lunches at the central plaza's tree-shaded outdoor tables.

Reston Town Center's vibrant street life and city-style features are the result of careful planning and design over the last 20 years. In fact, these features—compact design, the mix of uses, pedestrian amenities, and a shared parking arrangement allowing more space to be given people than cars—were only made possible by an extensive rezoning process that took Fairfax County three years. The result is classic urban appeal, as well as such suburban characteristics as easy automobile access and plentiful free parking.

The heart of Reston Town Center.

The City of Reston:
A Planned Community

To understand Reston Town Center, it is important first to learn about the history of the larger community of Reston, located 18 miles west of Washington, D.C., along the road leading to Dulles International Airport. This corridor is now the center of the booming northern Virginia high tech-industry and its notoriously out-of-control sprawl. However, when Reston was planned for the then-quiet rural area in the 1960s, its developer, Robert E. Simon Jr., envisioned something quite different: a unique "satellite city."

Simon's vision was to create seven European-style villages of 10,000 residents each, open to all races, with housing for all income levels and shops, parks, and work-places, as well as a "town center district" with the density, vitality, and symbolic character of a city.

Unfortunately, Simon had to sell the development rights because of financial problems, and his vision was never fully realized. By the 1980s, Reston did have some pedestrian-friendly and village-like neighborhoods containing various housing types, but it also had many large, single-family residential sections that resemble classically sprawling suburban developments. It still lacked a center.

Twenty Years Later: Reston Town Center

Considering that an urban core was planned for the city of Reston from its very beginning, it might be surprising that the development of Reston Town Center only began more than 20 years after the city's first residential neighborhoods were built. However, a certain critical mass of residential and daytime population was necessary to convince investors to support an ambitious shopping, employment, and entertainment center. By the late 1980s, this mass was there, and the first phase of Reston Town Center began.

It also took time to assemble a development team and to agree on a clear vision for Reston Town Center. Mobil Oil's (later ExxonMobil's) Reston Land Company (RLC), the community's master developer from 1978 to the mid-1990s, decided to recruit a partner with experience in developing sophisticated mixed-use projects. In 1984, RLC chose Himmel/ MKDG as co-developer and the two formed a general partnership known as Reston Town Center Associates. The winning design for the first phase was submitted by RTKL Associates, Inc. in 1984.

An earlier RTKL plan had been revised after an independent review challenged

A shopping street in Reston Town Center.

the design and development team to make a clearer decision about whether the project should be urban or suburban, and then to give greater emphasis and definition to the chosen direction. The choice was to make Reston Town Center as urban as possible. With that mandate, Reston Town Center broke new ground, as there was no previous example of a similarly ambitious plan to construct an urban core within an already built, low-density suburb.

The Crowds Gather

Reston Town Center has not only succeeded in fulfilling Simon's original vision as the heart of Reston, much loved and well used by residents, but it has also evolved into a regional attraction. There is nothing quite like it elsewhere in northern Virginia's suburbs.

The central public plaza—Fountain Square, named after its 20-foot tall bronze and marble fountain—is full of people year round. Listening to the sound of cascading water, workers and visitors can rest and eat at scattered tables under the shade of trees. During the lunch hour, tables fill quickly. Entrances and varied setbacks give the impression of a

PRINCIPALS

Developers: Reston Land Corporation (subsidiary of Mobil Land Development Corporation); Himmel & Co.; Equity Office Properties Trust; Terrabrook
Design: RTKL Associates; Sasaki Associates, Inc.
Public sector: Fairfax County

city that has evolved over time, and wide sidewalks, benches, and large trees encourage people to stroll around. Outdoor sculptures entertain the eye and mind. In the winter, families enjoy the popular ice skating rink; on summer evenings, free concerts draw crowds.

Shoppers come to visit more than 40 diverse shops. Most are national chains that have begun to venture out from the malls to experiment with "Main Street" locations. They include, for example, the Gap, Ann Taylor, Banana Republic, Pottery Barn, and Williams-Sonoma. Interestingly, attracting retailers to Reston Town Center was initially a challenge—it was misleadingly classified, for lack of enough similar suburban developments, as an "anchorless mall"—but those who came can now attest that they made a wise business decision. The shops are doing very well indeed, as are the dozen specialty restaurants.

Reston Town Center is also proving popular with other types of business. Such major companies as Apple Computers, MCI, Rolls Royce, and Reuters America have chosen to come to this central location. One of the newer tenants is Andersen Consulting (now Accenture), which leased a 16-story office tower.

An Island of Smart Growth

Reston Town Center has attractive smart-growth features—such as walkability, a variety and concentration of uses, and an active street life. But can this relatively small, urbane island in a mostly car-dependent, low-density suburban area have a real impact on environmental concerns?

The answer appears to be yes, even though the area lacks a major rail transit stop. A recent traffic study conducted by Wells & Associates, a planning and engineering firm, indicates that Reston Town Center generates close to 50 percent fewer automobile trips than would ordinarily be expected in a comparably sized suburban development—an encouraging, maybe even surprising, finding. The study found that the synergy among different uses, such as shopping, entertainment, and work, was a significant reason for these traffic reductions. For example, 70 percent of evening restaurant patronage is generated by pedestrians coming from within Reston Town Center. Similarly, 40 percent of the movie patrons and up to 15 percent of the retail patrons are generated internally.

Other factors identified by the study were the concentration of uses and the public transportation system. Reston Town Center, now the community's downtown, has a greater concentration of jobs than the typical suburban office park, which enables more workers to participate in van- and car pools. And the frequent bus service that connects the core to the rest of Reston and the Washington, D.C., Metro subway system also contributes to reducing automobile dependence.

These very encouraging findings indicate that even a relatively isolated smart-growth development can confer significant benefits. Not only has Reston Town Center helped to define Reston and give the community a pulsating heart, but it has also allowed suburbanites to take at least a few of their daily trips without cars. And that is no small feat.

PROJECT DATA

Initial Phase (1990):
- 20 acres
- 40 shops
- 12 cafes and restaurants
- 1 cinema
- 520,000 sq. ft. office space
- 514-room Hyatt Regency

At completion:
- 85 acres
- 300–400,000 sq. ft. retail space
- 2 million sq. ft. office space
- 1100 hotel rooms
- 600 residential units

TIMELINE

1962: County approves Reston plan   **1964:** First "village" built   **1981:** Planning for Town Center begins   **1984:** RTCA formed ; rezoning process begins   **1986:** Winning plan chosen   **1987:** Rezoning process ends   **1990:** Phase I opens   **Mid-1990s:** Terrabrook purchases Reston Town Center

THIRD STREET COTTAGES
LANGLEY, WASHINGTON

Many think of smart-growth developments as large-scale projects comprising scores if not hundreds of homes, frequently with shops and offices built in. But the values and principles that smart growth embraces can be applied to even the smallest of projects. Indeed, it is important to do so, for some communities may be presented with more small opportunities than large ones.

A POCKET-SIZED ENCLAVE OF SMART GROWTH

Just three blocks from the center of Langley, Washington, sits Third Street Cottages, an award-winning community of eight detached cottages placed around a common garden, covering less than an acre. Third Street Cottages is the first development of its kind, using an innovative zoning code that allows higher densities for smaller homes surrounding a common area. The development is part of an effort to increase residential density while retaining the charming character of the area.

Sitting in Sprawl's Path

A town of approximately 1,000 people, Langley is located on Whidbey Island, an hour away from downtown Seattle, in Puget Sound. Langley is not really a suburb. Not yet. So far, Whidbey Island, which is accessible only by ferry, has been spared the worst effects of suburban sprawl. But its proximity to Seattle and Everett, another fast-growing city, have put it in sprawl's path.

In an effort to preserve this rural character, the Island County government first imposed a minimum lot requirement of five acres. Unfortunately, had the opposite effect, spawning what Jim Soules, Third Street Cottages' developer, calls "five-acre ranchettes" that cut up

Third Street Cottages with community garden.

and divide the land, virtually guaranteeing sprawl. The community grew increasingly worried.

In response to the growing threat of sprawl, and in an effort to meet state urban growth and housing goals, the city of Langley's Growth Management Committee and the Planning Advisory Board established new conditions for land-use planning. Future revisions to the land-use code had to retain and enhance Langley's village character, by fostering strong neighborhoods and expanding the options for detached and affordable housing.

Using these criteria, Langley adopted the Cottage Housing Development (CHD) Zoning Ordinance in 1995. The CHD allows detached homes at twice the previous allowable density in single-family zones—up to 15 homes per acre. The ordinance encourages small houses of no more than 650 square feet on the first floor and no more than a total of 975 square feet. Each home must be adjacent to a common area, and parking spaces must be hidden from the street. Jim Soules points out that the CHD provision and the development respond to a major shift in demographics that is taking place across America. Most American households (about 58 percent) consist of one or two people, but the majority of detached housing is built for families.

Third Street Cottages, the community's first CHD project, offers an alternative to the usual townhouses, condominiums, and apartments typically available for singles and couples. The project, which was completed in January 1998 by Soules and architect Ross Chapin, is a successful integration of infill and compactness, built on a vacant parcel in the heart of Langley at a density of 12 development units per acre (DU/acre) on a site previously zoned at 6 DU/acre.

Sustainability and Community

"Sustainability is the key here," Chapin told reporter Judy Hammond. "When you build houses with care, people tend to put care back into them and they will last longer."[10] Indeed, all of the building materials used in the project were environmentally sound. No old-growth wood was used, and the whitewashed, wood-paneled walls are reclaimed Sitka spruce that was on its way to the pulp mill to make toilet paper. The builders did not use any drywall at any point in the construction.

While the interior space of each cottage was limited to 975 square feet, the developers did everything they could to make the houses feel spacious. In the living rooms, the ceilings are at least nine feet tall, and large windows and skylights create an open feeling. Walk-in closets, built-in shelves, and attics provide plenty of storage space. Seating alcoves, bay windows, and covered porches add additional functional space.

The development team also took particular care to create a sense of community at Third Street Cottages. They placed parking away from the houses so that a person coming to the cottages must first enter a courtyard. Mailboxes are clustered in a kiosk, inviting neighbors to stop and chat while getting their mail. Front porches and kitchen windows overlook the courtyard, creating a sense of security.

The courtyard is the heart of the small development. Neighbors work together in the garden or pick fruit from the old trees that were preserved during construction. They gather for parties at the workshop or trade tips in the cottages' collective tool shed. Decisions about the property are made by all of the residents. These group decisions range from choosing a communal barbecue grill to hiring someone to weed the garden.

In addition to fostering a sense of community, Soules and Chapin also provided residents with a sense of privacy. In front of each cottage is a swinging gate opening into a private yard. Each yard is bordered by a low fence and flowerbed. From the gate, a walkway leads to the steps up to the porch. The developers also positioned windows carefully within the cottages in order to ensure privacy.

Despite their similarities in design, each cottage has its own character. Flowerboxes and private gardens, for example, express the styles of the owners. Perhaps most expressive of all are the names the owners have given their cottages. Faith Smith, for example, calls hers Hale Ici Molokini, Hawaiian for "little house of many connections." "I grew up in wartime Maui, in a small cottage like this one," she told *The Seattle Times*. "This place reminds me of that very tight community where everyone kept an eye on each other."[11]

PRINCIPALS

Developer: Jim Soules of The Cottage Company
Design: Ross Chapin of Ross Chapin Architects
Public sector: City of Langley Growth Management Committee; Langley Planning Advisory Board

A Successful Model

Clearly, others wanted to be a part of that tight community, as well. The homes in Third Street Cottages sold quickly for $140,000 to

$150,000 each. In fact, five of the eight were sold before construction was completed. The first cottages were occupied in January 1998.

PROJECT DATA
- ▶ Detached homes: 8
- ▶ Maximum floor area: 975 sq. ft.
- ▶ Total development area: 0.67 acre

The project has received widespread local praise, as well as an award from *Sunset* magazine. Planners, developers, architects, and activists from other communities have visited. Several Puget Sound cities are considering adopting a CHD zoning provision like Langley's, and Soules and Chapin have gone on to develop more cottage projects around Whidbey and other parts of the area. For example, construction is now under way for the Greenwood Avenue Cottages in Shoreline, Washington, with completion expected in late 2001.

The owners of Third Street cottages are all conscious of sustainable living. Almost all of them own only one automobile, and most walk the three blocks to the village center of Langley to do their shopping. Peggy Moe, owner of the cottage named Pears and Cherries, told the *Seattle Times,* "Everyone here shares a belief that sustainability is an important value. We have to start taking responsibility for the earth's dwindling resources by taking a look at how we live."[12]

VILLAGE GREEN
LOS ANGELES, CALIFORNIA

At first glance, the Village Green residential development appears unexceptional: 77 small new homes plunked down in the ubiquitous suburban disarray of north Los Angeles. Further inspection, however,

SMART, SUSTAINABLE, AND AFFORDABLE RESIDENTIAL DEVELOPMENT

reveals a project that speaks to compelling needs for more sustainable forms of development.

In particular, Village Green responds to the rapidly growing need for moderately priced homes in the expensive Los Angeles market. An infill development next to a commuter rail station and bus transfer point, it offers a pleasant residential environment and convenient travel options, as well as state-of-the art energy systems. Its combination of affordability and green features, as well as its revitalization of the neighborhood, have attracted national attention.

Changes in the San Fernando Valley

Village Green occupies an 18-acre site in the San Fernando Valley at the northern edge of the city of Los Angeles. Even after the tide of development emanating from central Los Angeles swept north in the 1940s and 1950s, the owners of the site continued to farm it for many years. But, as the once-rural valley became more and more quintessentially suburban, farming became less and less attractive. The few farms that remained were soon surrounded by suburban growth and became ripe for infill development.

At the same time, the community around the site had begun to falter. The typically small houses in the nearby neighborhoods gradually came to display signs of wear and tear, although a few clusters of new housing

Affordable housing in Village Green.

THE LEE GROUP, INC.

brightened the area. By 1990, census figures showed that just over half of the households in the census tract were classified as low income.

Despite its lack of affluence, the area continued to offer many conveniences, providing a number of facilities for residents near the transit station: a child care center next door, several clusters of shops on surrounding main streets, an elementary school and a regional park within half a mile, and three other elementary schools, a senior high school, two libraries, and a post office within a mile's radius. The area remained livable and had bred a sense of community among its mostly Latino residents.

Meanwhile, the site's owners waited for an attractive purchase offer. One developer proposed a 300-unit project that fell victim to litigation over financial issues. Residents living nearby did not support the concept anyway, in part because of worries about traffic. Although some streets bordering the site were only half paved, traffic congestion was already a problem: trains on the Metrolink rail line crossed streets at grade, periodically interrupting traffic flows. During rush hours, buses and automobiles clogged the transit terminal and adjoining park-and-ride lot. Neighbors feared that additional traffic would spill over from new development onto local streets and worried about losing walking access through the site to the station and nearby schools.

Still, community residents realized that development could help rescue the area from what seemed to be a continuing downward slide. The challenge was to attract an appealing development that fit into the neighborhood.

Targeting Community Needs

The Lee Group and Braemar Urban Ventures, two firms that have been building homes in the Los Angeles area for more than 40 years, formed a joint venture to address this challenge. They proposed a development of single-family houses reflecting the scale and style of existing homes, with common green space in addition to small individual lots. The new homes would be priced to be affordable to families with annual incomes as low as $60,000.

From previous experience, the developers anticipated that most homebuyers would already live within five miles of the site and would be seeking to upgrade from renting to homeownership or from apartments to single-family homes. The project was organized as a condominium to allow decreases in lot sizes and street widths, which saved construction costs per unit and helped keep the homes affordable. This also made the neighborhood more compact, convenient, and efficient.

Jay Stark, the developers' project manager, expected relatively little trouble in obtaining approvals for Village Green, despite its overlapping of two municipalities—Los Angeles and San Fernando—and somewhat unconventional design. He says he knew that Los Angeles wanted this kind of higher-density development around rail stations, and that prospects for new affordable housing would be welcomed by the community. Stark also believed that the smart-growth features of the project would appeal to many residents.

Even so, Stark launched a vigorous eight-week campaign to inform residents of adjoining neighborhoods about the benefits of the proposed development. At community meetings, Stark described development plans and showed site designs and illustrations of the proposed housing. Following the meetings, the project's public relations assistant toured the surrounding neighborhoods and gathered more than 500 signatures in favor of the project; the signatures were later submitted to the two city councils.

Energy-Efficiency Features

The Lee-Braemar partnership decided early in the development process to explore opportunities for energy efficiency offered by the federal government's Partnership for Advanced Technology Housing (PATH) program, initiated in 1998 by the U.S. Departments of Energy and Housing and Urban Development. Their exploration was successful indeed: Village Green became the country's first PATH project. President Bill Clinton announced the program's initiation at the development's groundbreaking ceremony.

As part of the PATH program, a technical team sponsored by the two federal agencies recommended a number of design features

A quiet street in Village Green.

that would reduce energy consumption, and approximately 90 percent of their recommendations were adopted. As a result, Village Green's PATH houses are constructed with outstanding energy-efficiency features: steel and specially engineered wood wall frames that allow more room for insulation; environmentally superior cellulose insulation; dual-glazed insulating windows; and heating and cooling ducts placed within conditioned spaces of the house rather than the attic.

In addition, most of the homes in Village Green are designed to be equipped with photovoltaic cells to generate solar energy. These solar systems produce approximately 3,000 kilowatt-hours of electric power annually, meeting up to 90 percent of each home's electricity demand. Homes are also designed with energy-efficient light fixtures to further reduce energy consumption. Among still other green features, the homes' natural-gas-fueled space and water heating systems are more energy efficient than their electric counterparts, and the gas-powered air-conditioning system will last twice as long as conventional electric models. Energy-efficient appliances include water-saving washing machines and gas-powered clothes dryers.

PRINCIPALS

Developers: Lee Group; Braemar Urban Ventures
Design: Van Tilburg, Banvard & Soderbergh
Public sector: Fannie Mae's American Communities Fund and Partnership for Advanced Technology Housing (PATH)

Obtaining Financial Backing

Village Green is a $25-million project. From the beginning, the developers were prepared to invest some of their own funds, but they still needed substantial additional resources. Some of Village Green's smart-growth features—its moderately priced homes, infill site, and added construction costs for energy efficiency—portended potential obstacles to securing the necessary financing from conventional investors.

Fortunately, the project attracted the attention of the federal mortgage institution Fannie Mae, whose American Communities Fund (ACF) invests capital in projects that may lack sufficient appeal to traditional sources of funding but promise to revitalize neighborhoods. Judging Village Green to be such a project, ACF agreed to invest $2.5 million—to be repaid through revenues from housing sales—to finance part of the land purchase. Stark says that ACF's involvement "validated the project" in the eyes of both investors and homebuyers.

Village Green is taking shape as of this writing. The first phase, including the village green itself and 19 homes, was completed as scheduled. The three- and four-bedroom homes range from 1,400 to 1,700 square feet, including a two-car garage. Lots of approximately 3,000 square feet were arranged along narrow streets, yielding a density slightly higher than ten units per acre. Sidewalks and trees make the streets inviting to pedestrians. The central village green now also serves as a link between adjoining neighborhoods and the transit station. Along the site's edge, homefronts are turned outward to the neighborhood rather than inward to a closed-off environment.

Village Green home prices are $165,000 to $185,000, a notch higher than prices of older homes in the area but lower than most newer homes. They have elicited a great deal of interest from homebuyers. All 19 built units are occupied, and the additional 58 homes now under construction have already been sold.

Our discussion of Village Green was adapted with permission from Douglas R. Porter's article "L.A. Green," which appeared in the October 2000 edition of Urban Land.

Smart Conservation

*A nation deprived of its liberty may win it, a nation
divided may unite, but a nation whose natural resources
are destroyed must inevitably pay the penalty of poverty,
degradation, and decay.*

    —Gifford Pinchot, founder, U.S. Forest Service

As our preceding chapters illustrate, solving sprawl is fundamentally about planning and building new development in smart ways that use land efficiently, provide transportation options, put people within easy and convenient reach of their daily tasks, make good use of existing civic resources, and foster a sense of community for all parts of society. The stories in those chapters show that smart growth works, that as a society we can accomplish these things with a more thoughtful and deliberate approach to how we grow. The result, as we have documented, is a wealth of environmental and social benefits.

But solving sprawl is not just about how to develop properly. It is also about deciding where to develop and, importantly, where *not* to develop—about deciding what in our landscape and our heritage must be preserved for future generations. It is about thoughtfully respecting nature instead of ruthlessly obliterating it.

There can be little doubt that the American public is ready to keep sprawling development out of our natural landscape and farmland. In a September 2000 poll of a representative sample of adults nationwide, 83 percent of those responding favored the establishment of "zones for green space, farming, and forests outside existing cities and suburbs that would be off limits to developers." In addition, 77 percent of those responding in the same poll, conducted for the coalition

Smart Growth America, favored the use of "tax dollars to buy land for more parks and open space and to protect wildlife."

A variety of large-scale tools exist for protecting farmland, wildlife habitat, watersheds, and scenic vistas. These include a statewide network of forest and farm zones, such as those pioneered in Oregon; statewide rural preservation incentive programs, such as those recently enacted under Governor Glendening's leadership in Maryland; regional habitat conservation plans that restrict development, such as the one in Clark County, Nevada, designed to address the needs of some 79 species; and ambitious programs to purchase land or conservation easements, such as the $14 million program to save New Jersey farmland launched by Governor Christine Todd Whitman before her appointment as administrator of the federal Environmental Protection Agency.

Our book, however, is less about policies than about specific on-the-ground successes. In this chapter, we want to show how communities have managed to maintain cherished parts of their landscape despite development pressures. As a result, our stories tend to focus not on large-scale programs but on very localized techniques and strategies that have been successful and that provide models that communities elsewhere can emulate. Many of them represent achievements that were initiated or substantially assisted by ordinary citizens concerned about the spread of sprawl in or near their communities; several illustrate the valuable role that land trusts can play in facilitating preservation transactions; and some have been the direct result of enlightened leadership in local government.

Preserving Farmland

Two of our examples illustrate outstanding countywide initiatives to protect farmland. Maryland's Montgomery County Agricultural Preserve is the country's most successful farmland preservation program, using a variety of techniques to maintain an intact, working landscape just outside the suburbs of Washington, DC. Pennsylvania's Chester County Comprehensive Plan offers an example of a particularly outstanding master-planning effort. Among its features are urban growth boundaries—an increasingly popular and often (but not always, as we discuss) successful technique for containing development within designated zones.

Safeguarding Waterways

A second category consists of efforts to protect especially important parts of local waterways. These include Georgia's Chattahoochee

River National Recreation Area, which also provides an example of how urban conservation efforts are frequently just as important as those in rural areas; in addition, the Chattahoochee case shows how the federal government can join with states and localities to help save locally important resources. Barton Creek Wilderness Park in Austin, Texas, is another example of an important in-town waterway preservation effort. Rural examples of successful efforts to protect water resources include North Carolina's Mountain Island Lake and Michigan's Pearl Lake.

Creating Greenways and Greenbelts

Greenways and greenbelts comprise corridors of connected conservation areas. When planned and assembled wisely, such corridors not only save scenic vistas and natural recreation areas but also provide valuable migration routes for wildlife. The greenbelt in Boulder, Colorado, remains a testament to one of the country's first smart-growth efforts; it also provides an example of in-town preservation and of an urban growth boundary. The Chattahoochee River National Recreation Area, mentioned above, is now a 48-mile corridor of protected land that, when completed, will stretch for 180 miles through north Georgia. The Mountains to Sound Greenway protects a scenic corridor for more than 100 miles through the state of Washington's majestic Cascade Mountains.

Protecting Unique Resources

It is a sad fact of American development that sprawl can destroy not just scenery or habitat, not just forests or farms, but also our heritage. In solving sprawl with smart growth, we must be attentive to the conservation of historic resources along with those that we think of as "natural." Our story of Maryland's Antietam Battlefield is a splendid example of exactly that. Finally, transcending category boundaries is the example of California's beautiful Coast Dairies, saved through the efforts of a large partnership of nonprofit organizations and all levels of government, and which preserves farmland, coastal access for recreation, scenic vistas, and wildlife habitat all at once.

ANTIETAM BATTLEFIELD
NEAR SHARPSBURG, MARYLAND

Sharpsburg, Maryland, is only an hour-and-a-half's drive from the booming metropolitan areas of Washington and Baltimore, and even closer to the city of Frederick and the rapidly developing I-270 high-tech corridor. But waves of development did not reach Sharpsburg until the 1980s. In fact, as late as 1980, its rolling hills, working farms, and eighteenth- and nineteenth-century stone houses, barns, and bridges looked remarkably similar to how they appeared to Union and Confederate soldiers on September 17, 1862, when the Battle of Antietam was fought on its grounds.

A CIVIL WAR BATTLEFIELD SAVED FROM ENCROACHING SPRAWL

Known as the "bloodiest day" in American history, the Battle of Antietam claimed more than 23,000 men killed, wounded, and missing in a single day. It ended General Robert E. Lee's first invasion of the North and provided President Abraham Lincoln with the victory he needed to announce the Emancipation Proclamation.

An act of Congress established Antietam National Battlefield as a national park on August 30, 1890. Today, the Congressionally authorized boundary encompasses 3,250 acres. However, the fighting took place on 8,000 acres. In the 1980s, as the Sharpsburg area came under growing development pressure, the remaining 4,000 acres of the historic battlefield, unprotected by the federal government, fell under increasing threat.

Antietam Battlefield.

Development Squeezes Historic Site

In the late 1980s, two housing subdivisions, Confederate Hills and Battlefield Knolls, were being built on the west side of Sharpsburg. In addition, high-priced homes on hilltops northwest of Sharpsburg and

GRANT DEHART

west of the battlefield started popping up. Some developers also speculated in farmland for tract housing. Some of these development plans would have affected especially significant historic spots. For example, the Grove Farm, where President Lincoln met General George McClellan after the battle, was seriously threatened. Forty acres of the farm were zoned by the county for a ten-lot residential subdivision; an additional five-acre parcel was slated for construction of an American Legion Hall; and 20 acres were zoned for a motel and a shopping center.

By 1990, the National Trust for Historic Preservation had placed the Antietam area among its most endangered historic sites in the country. Although some initial grants from the National Trust and the state's Maryland Environmental Trust helped with initial preservation efforts—enabling the acquisition of 40 acres of the Grove Farm—the 1990–1991 economic recession dried up further state funds for rural and historic preservation.

There had been some weak previous efforts to conserve the landscape around Antietam. A county advisory committee had proposed a change in zoning to require a three-acre minimum lot size, but the proposal died because of landowner opposition. (It also would have done little to prevent sprawl.) There was also talk of expanding the boundaries of the battlefield park by condemnation and acquisition of additional land, but this idea, too, did not materialize.

A new and more promising opportunity came after 1991, however, when Congress enacted the Intermodal Surface Transportation Efficiency Act (ISTEA), requiring that a percentage of Maryland's federal highway funds be dedicated to "transportation enhancements," including historic preservation and scenic easements near roadsides, along with other eligible categories. In February 1992, the state of Maryland pledged to dedicate $5 million of its allocated ISTEA funds to acquire Civil War sites and greenways, and to match this amount with its own open-space funds.

The first meeting with Sharpsburg-area property owners, who had opposed the previous efforts, took place soon after. State officials explained their plans to buy easements on a strictly voluntary basis, with independent, fair-market-value appraisals. They pledged to buy land in fee only when the owner would not sell an easement, and to allow lands to be farmed after easements had been conveyed to the state. Several people in the room, including formerly vocal property rights advocates, expressed an interest in signing up to begin negotiating easements. The community that had been resistant to regulation was ready to embrace a program of incentives.

A Victory Without Casualties

Over 80 percent of all the property owners contacted chose to participate in the program. To date, the state has used its funding, along with the ISTEA allocation, to purchase or acquire conservation easements on properties totaling over 4,000 acres. There is now more land protected outside the National Park Service boundary than within. And still more will be preserved: a new statewide preservation initiative, the Rural Legacy Program, has given the county an additional $3.1 million to continue buying easements around Antietam and on Red Hill, the forested backdrop to the battlefield. Thanks to these efforts, residents and visitors can now see a clear line where sprawling development ends and undisturbed rural land begins.

PRINCIPALS
Public sector: Maryland Environmental Trust; Maryland Department of Agriculture; U.S. Department of Transportation
Nonprofit: National Trust for Historic Preservation

Some 130 years after the Civil War, residents of Antietam won a different kind of battle, against encroaching sprawl. But this time, there were no casualties, only beneficiaries. Thanks to forward-looking state policies, and an innovative federal program, family farms can continue being operated profitably, while visitors today can see the entire Antietam Battlefield much as it was when history was made there.

BARTON CREEK WILDERNESS PARK
AUSTIN, TEXAS

In the nineteenth century, Austin was cattle country. But, by the end of the twentieth century, the city was home to a rapidly increasing human population drawn to its beauty, lively cultural scene, and pleasant climate. Greater Austin's population tripled between 1970 to 1996. High-tech

FARSIGHTED LEADERS PRESERVE THEIR CITY'S GREEN SPACES

companies in particular focused on the region, seeking an educated workforce and the high quality of life that would keep employees happy.

But soon that quality of life came into question. Like many attractive and livable places, Austin fell victim to its own success, as the values that had lured people to the city were undermined by rapid growth and unsound development. Citizens and government officials realized the need for a more thoughtful, balanced approach. Instead of allowing development to proceed unchecked, the old cattle town took the bull by the horns. Austin redoubled its efforts to protect its beautiful natural areas.

Wildlife haven and relaxing wilderness near downtown Austin.

Green Space, Clean Water Threatened

One of Austin's more unusual features is a spring-fed swimming hole, Barton Springs Pool, located within the city limits. Since the 1830s when a settler, Billy Barton, began charging locals to swim there, generations of residents have enjoyed the pool, braving its chilly waters or relaxing along its shores. Each year, a quarter of a million people visit Barton Springs Pool.

After Austin's growth spurt, this much-loved resource began showing signs of distress. By the 1980s, upstream development was affecting the water's clarity. Local officials sometimes had to close the swimming hole after heavy rains, which washed in runoff and raised bacteria levels. A turning point came in 1990, when a new subdivision with three golf courses, sprawling across thousands of acres, was proposed for Barton Creek upstream of Barton Springs

Pool. Concerned citizens held a vigil at the springs, and hundreds protested the development at a public hearing that lasted 13 hours. The city council denied the permit and began working on new regulations to protect the Barton Springs area.

But even more was at stake than this oasis of green. Barton Springs is part of the Edwards Aquifer, which not only meets the needs of the region's wildlife but is also the sole source of drinking water for more than 1.5 million people, including residents of Austin and San Antonio. Because this segment of the aquifer is so small and porous, it is particularly vulnerable to pollution.

Austin had a history of varied efforts to safeguard water quality. In 1970, the city started monitoring local lakes and creeks and, beginning in 1979, it passed five local water-quality ordinances—the first focused on Barton Creek. They were superseded in 1986 by the Comprehensive Watersheds Ordinance, which restricted development in the city. But concerns remained about the limits of regulation. In the five years after the comprehensive ordinance passed, 86 percent of Austin's new development failed to comply with the standards but was built anyway, largely because of variances or grandfather clauses. Pressure grew for acquiring land as a way to protect the city's waters.

Protecting Austin's Open Spaces

Austinites had already taken steps to acquire some of the region's open space. In the 1970s, voters approved bonds to acquire parkland. The most prominent result was the 800-acre Barton Creek greenbelt,

which included Barton Springs Pool. But the city stalled on other purchases, and several adjoining parcels became subdivisions. As development encroached, right up to the greenbelt's edges, it became increasingly clear that additional land around Barton Creek needed protection.

In addition to its famous pool, the Barton Creek area boasts cliffs, virgin forest, and two waterfalls. Evidence points to habitation in Barton Creek Canyon 11,000 years ago, and some archeological sites remain. Whitetail deer, fox, squirrels, and cottontail rabbits have made the area home, along with such rare species as the Black-capped vireo and the Golden-cheeked warbler, and rare plants like the Bracted twistflower.

In July, 1992, after studying the Barton Creek watershed, the Austin Parks and Recreation Department and the National Park Service recommended adding 1,050 acres of public land to the existing greenbelt. The resulting urban wilderness park would preserve the

SNAPSHOT: **THREATENED WILDLIFE NEAR AUSTIN**

Notwithstanding the preservation success of Barton Creek, and an earnest attempt to create a larger preserve around Austin to protect endangered species habitat, all is not well for wildlife in the Hill Country. Indeed, of all the habitat conservation plans in the country reviewed by the nonprofit group Defenders of Wildlife in 1998, "the most disappointing example" was the Balcones Canyonlands Conservation Plan for Travis County, which includes Austin.

The Balcones plan went through a long and contentious planning process that spanned eight years. The most controversial part of the plan was a biological advisory team's recommendations for preserves for two endangered bird species. According to the team's calculations, this would require 130,000 acres of preserves (Travis County is 648,000 acres), after taking into account decline in habitat quality due to edge effects, urbanization and habitat fragmentation. The final design, however, consisted of only 30,428 acres distributed in seven preserve units, even if all anticipated funding is realized.

More positively, the plan was also instrumental in the establishment of Balcones Canyonlands National Wildlife Refuge, where management for significant numbers of the endangered birds will enhance populations. But, while the acreage of the preserve and the wildlife refuge together includes many large, relatively unfragmented habitat patches for the birds, and while habitat management will slow habitat degradation due to public use, the preserve design still falls far short of original, biologically-based expectations. Indeed, analysts at Defenders of Wildlife note that the plan may not sustain the population viability of the golden-cheeked warbler, the primary focus of the preserve system.

area's natural values while offering Austinites new opportunities for boating, biking, birding, and other outdoor activities. In addition, the park would provide a much-needed buffer against future development, helping to defend water quality in the Edwards Aquifer. The proposal quickly gained support, and a bond issue to raise funds for purchasing the land was placed on the ballot.

August 1992 was a significant month for Austin's environment and its citizens' health. Voters demonstrated their support for open space and water quality by approving the bond act, which authorized $20 million in land purchases for the new Barton Creek Wilderness Park. On the same day, they approved the issuance of an additional $22 million in bonds to preserve habitat in the Balcones Canyonlands, and they approved the Save Our Springs (SOS) water quality initiative, a measure aimed at protecting the Barton Creek watershed by controlling runoff. The SOS initiative was later weakened by the legislature, which exempted developments whose planning—no matter how preliminary—had begun before SOS was enacted.

Next came the work of buying the land around Barton Creek. The city was initially able to appropriate only $1 million, a sum that would not go far toward meeting the goal of acquiring 1,050 acres. The nonprofit Trust for Public Land stepped in, negotiating with the owners of the properties slated for the park and using its own funds to purchase more property, more quickly, than the city could have done, keeping the acquisitions on track.

In 1993 and 1994, the trust bought several parcels of land, and Barton Creek Wilderness Park came together. By moving forward immediately, the trust was able to take advantage of favorable market conditions. (It has since sold the land to the city.) As a result, Austin was able to stretch its dollars much farther than

Scenic Barton Creek.

SAVE BARTON CREEK ASSOCIATION

SNAPSHOT: SMART GROWTH AND WATER QUALITY

Natural landscapes, such as forests, wetlands, and grasslands, are typically varied and porous. They trap rainwater and snowmelt and filter it into the ground slowly. When precipitation causes runoff, it tends to reach receiving waterways gradually. Cities and suburbs, by contrast, are characterized by large paved or covered surfaces that are impervious to rain. Instead of percolating slowly into the ground, storm water becomes trapped above these surfaces, accumulates, and runs off in large amounts into streams, lakes, and estuaries, picking up pollutants along the way. Along with increased water volume come sediment, pathogens, nutrients (such as nitrogen and phosphorous), heavy metals, pesticides, and nondegradable debris. As a result, there is a strong correlation between the amount of imperviousness in a drainage basin and the health of its receiving stream.

Sprawling land development extends pavement and associated runoff pollution into more and more watersheds. On-site measures to assist water quality, such as maximizing natural ground cover in individual lots, are overwhelmed by rooftops and especially the larger system of roadways and parking lots required to serve sprawl. Research shows that large-lot subdivisions increase imperviousness by 10 to 50 percent compared to cluster and traditional town developments with the same number of households, and that they deliver up to three times more sediment into waterways.

Smart growth protects watersheds by concentrating development efficiently within contained urban and growth areas. This allows rural areas to remain in low-density or resource-based land uses, and requires fewer roads and other impervious surfaces region-wide.

might otherwise have been possible. In less than two years, nearly 1,000 acres were purchased for the park.

A Continuing Commitment to Open Space

Austin has continued its activities to promote smart growth and protect natural areas. In 1998, the city adopted its Comprehensive Smart Growth Initiative. The city council designated the most sensitive third of the Austin region (including land that drains into Barton Springs) a Drinking Water Protection Zone; the remaining two-thirds became the Desired Development Zone. The aim is to draw development away from the protected areas and into the desired zones, where incentives would promote such smart-growth measures as pedestrian-friendly neighborhoods and placing new buildings near public transportation. Voters have passed bond initiatives to buy land within the protection zone and for open space generally.

Austin remains dominated by sprawl, unfortunately, but the conservation commitment begun with the protection of Barton Creek suggests that the community is doing something about it. Since 1990, the city has acquired more than 3,000 acres of parkland, more than 9,000 acres aimed at protecting endangered species, and about 15,000 acres for protecting water quality. Like many other observers, Ted Harrison, southwest regional director for the Trust for Public Land, calls Austin's approach visionary. The city, he says, "is among the most farsighted communities in the West when it comes to issues of land conservation and smart growth." Harrison points to surveys of new businesses and homeowners, according to which, he says, the city's "current economic boom is largely a function of the high quality of life, access to parks, and community cultural investments that the city has pursued during the past three decades."[1] In other words, Austin's commitment has not only helped preserve open space; it has also kept the economy humming and its quality of life high.

BOULDER'S GROWTH-CONTROL INITIATIVES

BOULDER, COLORADO

S ituated in one of the most beautiful places in the United States, Boulder, Colorado is surrounded by spectacular mountains and open prairie. Natural beauty abounds within the city as well, in an extensive network of parks and trails. Boulder also has a well-preserved historic downtown

CONTINUING ONE OF THE COUNTRY'S ORIGINAL SMART-GROWTH EFFORTS

that is home to numerous art galleries and restaurants. The University of Colorado adds to the city's vibrancy.

For a while after World War II, civic leaders worked hard to draw industry and residents to Boulder. They successfully lobbied for a highway to connect the city to Denver, 25 miles to the southeast. But, by the 1950s, Boulderites were turning a critical eye on the changing shape of their city. Boulder was on the edge of a painful dilemma: its beauty and quality of life were powerful lures, but they were also threatened by the resulting growth.

Boulder's preserved landscape.

Boulder was hardly the first city to face this paradox. But, in responding, it took steps whose vigor and creativity have rarely been matched. Other cities, like Seattle and Atlanta, have tried to contain sprawl—but only after it had already eaten up huge swaths of open space. In contrast, Boulder decided to *prevent* sprawl. Over the years, it has experimented with a variety of measures. Most have made a difference; a few have been dropped. But, overall, the city has been remarkably successful in remaining compact and preserving its open space.

Keeping Open Space Open

In 1960, 1.75 million people lived in Colorado. Thirty years later, the state had nearly 3.3 million residents. Much of this expansion took place among Boulder's neighbors in the front range of the Rockies, an area that has seen some of the country's fastest growth since the 1960s. Of course, Boulder itself grew too: from 1960 to 1990, its population more than doubled, from 37,000 to over

86,000. But while nearby areas simply let growth happen—and watched it turn into sprawl—Boulder took a series of aggressive steps to control how and where its growth would take place.

One of the most famous efforts came in 1959 when Boulder amended its charter to establish a "blue line" at an altitude of 5,780 feet. The line is the cutoff point for water and sewage services: above it, the city will not provide either. The measure has kept the city's western hills uncluttered and unspoiled. Boulderites were also the first Americans to tax themselves to buy open space. In 1967, city voters approved a sales tax whose revenues finance a purchasing program. Since then, the tax has raised more than $137 million, which has been used to preserve 30,000 acres of parks and open space; in 1999 alone, Boulder spent $18.6 million to save 2,168 acres.

The city has even been able to shape how some areas outside its borders grow. In 1978, in a joint effort with Boulder County, it developed the Boulder Valley Comprehensive Plan, which outlines desired land use both in the city and in adjacent areas.

A City with Sharp Edges

These measures—and many others—have had a dramatic effect. While its neighbors sprawled outward, Boulder stayed compact. Nearby Denver and Fort Collins saw landscape after landscape succumb to

the bulldozer. Boulder, meanwhile, protected tens of thousands of acres of open land on its edges.

In fact, through land purchases and easements, Boulder has now preserved an area twice the size of the city itself. This vast and beautiful greenbelt preserves the stunning vistas Boulder is famous for. It also provides unbroken wildlife habitat, sustaining the region's ecological integrity, while vastly reducing runoff and erosion. It offers virtually limitless opportunities for recreation. And it sets a clear boundary that defines where growth is appropriate. Thanks to its greenbelt, Boulder is a city of distinct edges. Growth is channeled inside its borders—where it is carefully managed.

In Boulder, most new growth takes place near existing development. This pattern saves money as well as land, since it allows new residents to use existing infrastructure instead of forcing the city to extend power lines, water systems, and other services. New residents are also able to take advantage of Boulder's excellent public transportation system, including the popular Hop and Skip shuttle buses. (Three new bus lines—named Jump, Leap, and Bound—were due in mid-2001.) In addition, Boulder has taken pains to echo the beauty of its surroundings in its city center. No resident is far from a bicycle trail or park. The city has also restored and enhanced its existing architecture.

SNAPSHOT: IS "SLOW GROWTH" ALSO "SMART"?

Along with its varied smart-growth efforts, Boulder has also experimented with measures designed to limit population increases. Such measures might best be classified as "slow" growth and have been initiated in other parts of the country as well. Perhaps the best-known example is Boulder's two percent annual ceiling on population growth, enforced by limiting the construction of new housing. Adopted by referendum in 1976, the cap was tightened to one percent in 1995.

These measures help keep residential population growth steady within a city's jurisdiction. But they tend to push growth elsewhere, frequently into open spaces or communities that lack their own measures to mitigate sprawl. They also sometimes fail to address commercial growth. In Boulder, office and retail development has soared—along with traffic. As jobs have been created for new workers in Boulder's commercial areas, the strain on nearby communities has grown.

Housing has become an issue within Boulder as well. Some people have blamed the city's slow-growth policies for creating a shortage of middle- and low-income housing. To its credit, Boulder is home to several innovative affordable housing developments, and the city has used a points system favoring multiple-family, low-income housing. Supporters of its policies also point to the city's generous package of assistance for lower-income residents.

In Boulder, planners are now addressing these issues squarely, and recognizing the need for more comprehensive approaches to economic growth and affordable housing. In fact, these issues have been major themes in the forthcoming update of the Boulder Valley Comprehensive Plan.

Lessons in Smart Growth

Boulder is a gracious host, frequently welcoming planners and civic leaders from other communities eager to learn about its smart-growth practices. These guests have the benefit of Boulder's decades of trial and error. But observers also are increasingly recognizing another lesson that Boulder teaches: the need for regional cooperation. Although, as noted, the city has had some success in this sphere, no one municipality—even one as diligent and creative as Boulder—can tackle sprawl on its own, and many of Boulder's neighbors have allowed precisely the kind of unchecked growth that Boulder itself has resisted. Unless the commitment to protect open space is shared across borders, there will always be the danger that sprawl will be displaced, not eliminated. (See accompanying discussion on slow growth.)

PRINCIPALS

Public sector: Open Space and Mountain Parks Department, City of Boulder; Planning Department, City of Boulder; Parks and Open Space Department, Boulder County; Land Use Department, Boulder County

Still, Boulder's biggest lesson is that communities *can* take a stand against sprawl. Open space can be protected, and development can be channeled to appropriate areas. Instead of letting development determine the contours of their city, Boulderites decided what kind of city they wanted. Their vision has kept Boulder beautiful, livable, compact, and green.

CHATTAHOOCHEE RIVER
NATIONAL RECREATION AREA
GWINNETT AND FORSYTH COUNTIES, GEORGIA

For generations, Georgia schoolchildren memorized Sidney Lanier's poem *Song of the Chattahoochee,* which celebrates the river's beauty and calm. Recently, however, the river has drawn attention not for its serenity, but for its woeful condition. The Chattahoochee has become one of the most polluted and endangered rivers in the United States.

RIVER SHORE PROTECTED IN THE MIDST OF RAPID GROWTH

The Chattahoochee runs 400 miles, from the Appalachian Mountains to the Gulf of Mexico. Like many rivers, it is paying the price of unchecked growth along its banks in the form of pollution and erosion. But the Chattahoochee has the distinction of flowing through one of the country's most egregious examples of sprawl: the greater Atlanta region. An estimated 60 percent of metropolitan Atlanta's natural areas disappeared in the last 25 years, and, by 1998, development in the area had become so spread out that Atlantans were driving more miles per person than residents of any other U.S. metropolitan area.

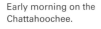
Early morning on the Chattahoochee.

Green Space for a Growing City

Sprawl has become a big issue in the Atlanta region, which is now trying to redirect its growth and keep more open space away from the bulldozer. In many ways, the evolution of the Chattahoochee River National Recreation Area is also the story of Atlantans' changing views. Created more than 20 years ago, the park never reached its intended size; many properties that were meant to be included wound up, instead, in developers' hands. But, today, politicians and governments at all levels are working with local citizens to enlarge and consolidate the park. Meanwhile, an ambitious effort to protect an even longer stretch of the Chattahoochee riverfront is meeting with great success.

The Chattahoochee River National Recreation Area hosts more than 3 million visitors annually, in some years drawing more people than even Yellowstone or the Lincoln Memorial. It's easy to see why the park is so popular. In the midst of a rapidly growing urban area, it provides a peaceful, green setting, home to fox, deer, beavers, herons, and osprey. People flock there to fish, hike, canoe, and raft—or sometimes simply to get away from the bustle and grime of the city.

The recreation area is metropolitan Atlanta's largest park. It was created in 1978 by Congress, which authorized a 6,300—acre park to embrace large tracts between Atlanta and Lake Lanier, an area that includes 48 miles of the Chattahoochee. The targeted area was raised to 6,800 acres in 1984.

But, 20 years after its creation, only 4,500 acres had been purchased for the recreation area and turned over to the National Park Service. Moreover, they lay in 16 separate and fragmented units, many of them miles apart from each other. Some of the remaining lands had been allowed to slip away, becoming subdivisions and office parks.

Yet, during those 20 years, attitudes about growth in the Atlanta region changed sharply.

> **SMART-GROWTH FEATURES**
> ▶ Critical riverfront protected from sprawl
> ▶ Metropolitan region's largest park consolidated
> ▶ Federal, state, and local agencies cooperate on plan
> ▶ Planning underway to extend the length of protected riverfront

One of the most rapidly-expanding cities in America was ready to change, and politicians of all stripes—and at all levels of government—were fighting to preserve open lands. "People are starving for their green space," Sally Bethea, executive director of the Upper Chattahoochee Riverkeeper told the magazine *Land and People.* "They want the green space because everything around them is turning into concrete."[2]

Political Leadership

In 1998, an unlikely champion of the park stepped forward: U.S. House of Representatives Speaker Newt Gingrich, who sponsored a bill to enlarge the Chattahoochee River National Recreation Area to 10,000 acres. The legislation failed to pass that year—it was attached to a larger proposal containing several controversial measures—but members of the Georgia delegation did secure a $25 million appropriation for acquiring land within the existing boundaries. Then, in 1999, under Representative Nathan Deal's sponsorship, the House approved the 10,000-acre bill. Georgia's senators, Paul Coverdell and

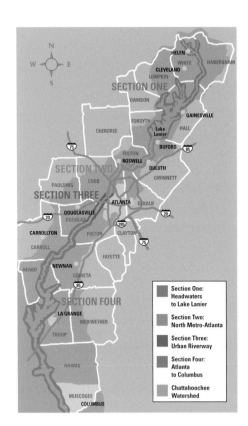

Sections of the protected Chattahoochee River.

Max Cleland, sponsored the Senate version, which passed in November. When President Bill Clinton signed the law in December 1999, the original plan for the park came back into reach. The greater acreage offered new opportunities to connect its fragmented sections and create the continuous corridor of green that had always been intended.

Since then, state and local governments have also acted on their own initiative to buy and protect green space within the park's authorized boundary. For instance, Gwinnett County is investing about $12 million, Forsyth County $1.5 million. The city of Roswell has spent $3 million and has committed to spending another $25 million to protect a seven-mile stretch.

The Trust for Public Land and other private groups have also stepped in, negotiating for a wide range of lands and holding them until government funding is actually appropriated. By January 2000, negotiations for 22 additional parcels within the park were already under way. By December 2000, an additional 800 acres had been acquired. All of this land will ultimately be managed by the National Park Service.

Beyond the Park

Meanwhile, efforts to protect an even longer stretch of the Chattahoochee continue to progress. The Trust for Public Land, the Upper Chattahoochee Riverkeeper, and many other local groups have joined forces with government officials and citizens to acquire additional land on both sides of the river. Their goal is to form a 500-foot-wide, unbroken greenway from the Chattahoochee's headwaters in the Appalachians to Columbus, Georgia. That is a 180-mile-long stretch.

Some land is being donated, some sold. Some is being swapped, with owners trading sensitive riverfront parcels for other properties more appropriate for development. Once again, the vision of Georgia's political leaders

PROJECT DATA

▶ 6,300 acres: original goal for area to be protected

▶ 4,500 acres: protected as of 1998

▶ 10,000 acres: goal of newly enacted legislation

has helped make the acquisitions possible. In 1998, River Care 2000, a preservation initiative launched by Governor Zell Miller, provided $15 million to the campaign. In 2000, Miller's successor, Roy Barnes, proposed a sweeping, statewide green-space program, asking for $20 million for land purchases along the Chattahoochee, as well as $30 million to help cities and counties buy land.

In pushing for the legislation, Barnes hammered home the connections among open space, livability, and economic growth. "This is all inextricably woven to attract people," he said in introducing the legislation to the general assembly. "To continue growth, you have to make sure that you do not destroy quality of life."[3]

PRINCIPALS

Public sector: Reps. Newt Gingrich and Nathan Deal; Senators Paul Coverdell and Max Cleland; Govs. Zell Miller and Roy Barnes; U.S. National Park Service; Gwinnett County; Forsyth County; city of Roswell

Nonprofit: Trust for Public Land; Upper Chattahoochee Riverkeeper

It's an argument that Georgians are taking to heart—in approving the legislation proposed by their governor, and in other efforts to keep the state's dwindling green spaces green. The Chattahoochee is benefiting immensely from these varied activities.

CHESTER COUNTY
COMPREHENSIVE PLAN
CHESTER COUNTY, PENNSYLVANIA

Chester County, in southeastern Pennsylvania, is one of the three original Pennsylvania counties created by state founder William Penn in 1682. It abounds with rolling hills, stream-filled valleys and woodlands, giant sycamores and wild-flowers, as well as horse farms, covered bridges, and beautiful old houses, some dating back to the 1700s.

A BOLD AND INNOVATIVE AGENDA FOR SAVING A LANDSCAPE FROM SPRAWL

The county also contains some particularly cherished landmarks of American history, including Brandywine Battlefield and Valley Forge National Historical Park. Agriculture flourishes there too: Chester County is home to about 1500 farms on about 175,000 acres, growing such crops as alfalfa, barley, and corn.

Sprawl Threatens Historic Farmland

But Chester County is far from exclusively rural. In fact, it is Pennsylvania's fastest-growing county. Its northern edge is already mostly suburban, and the remainder is directly in the path of sprawl, which is spreading from central Philadelphia, 30 miles east, and Wilmington, Delaware, just 18 miles south. From 1960 to 1995, the county's population nearly doubled and, from 1970 to 1995, more than 50,000 acres of land were developed—a greater amount than in the previous 300 years. From 1987 to 1992 alone, more than 12,000 acres of farmland were converted from agricultural use.

In 1995, county planners estimated that, if the pace continued, all of Chester County's farmland would be gone in less than 40 years. Other projections were equally sobering. An

Chester County farmland.

additional 80,000 people, needing 43,000 new housing units, were expected to move to the county over the next 25 years. If current development patterns continued, an additional 60,000 acres of land would be lost.

SMART-GROWTH FEATURES
- ▶ Regional approach to smart growth
- ▶ Extensive citizen involvement
- ▶ Identification of areas (suburban, urban) appropriate for future growth
- ▶ Urban growth boundaries to keep development compact and preserve open space

Chester County is not alone in facing these threats. But it is unusual in its response. Unlike many of their colleagues, the county's leaders have decided to do something about the sprawl that threatens the beauty and livability of their home.

Pennsylvania is not an easy place to launch a regional strategy for controlling growth. State laws allow counties to prepare comprehensive plans, but (as in many U.S. locations) zoning authority lies with city and town governments. For county officials who want to promote smart growth, it's a matter of convincing, not compelling: since they cannot impose growth controls, they have to find the right combination of incentives to bring local officials on board. Chester County has found this mix.

In 1995, the county set out to stem the loss of its farms, woods, and other open lands. To turn back the tide of sprawl, the Chester County Planning Commission began revising its comprehensive plan.

Balancing Preservation and Growth

From the start, the commission involved both citizens and local officials in the planning process, keeping them informed while soliciting their views. It used a newspaper insert to describe recent development patterns, explain the concerns, and gather the public's views. Respondents were clear about what they wanted: by a ten-to-one margin, they preferred denser, less sprawling development in targeted areas to the current haphazard patterns of growth.

PROJECT DATA
- ▶ 175,000 acres of farmland at stake
- ▶ 430,000 living in county
- ▶ 80,000 more people, 43,000 new homes projected for 2020

The commission also set up a 26-member policy committee, representing all regions of the county and varied interests. The committee identified areas and characteristics to preserve, as well as the places most suited for new development. The planning commission ran community design workshops, at which citizens explored their attitudes about visual qualities of rural, suburban, and urban landscapes. It held conferences and workshops that allowed

To Chester County's west lies Lancaster County, also home to farmland rich in history and agriculture. The experience in Lancaster—best known as the heart of Pennsylvania's Amish and other Plain Sect, sometimes called "Pennsylvania Dutch," communities—provides cause for both hope and concern.

On the bright side is the county's experience with conservation easements and similar techniques, which have preserved some 466 farms—covering more than 40,000 acres—throughout the county. That makes Lancaster's the second-largest farmland preservation program in the country, behind Maryland's Montgomery County (see our separate discussion of Montgomery's acclaimed program). But, at the same time, Lancaster County continues to lose about 1,000 acres of farmland to development each year, and guidelines for implementing growth boundaries have proved too weak to prevent large-lot development from occurring outside the boundaries. World Monuments Watch has placed Lancaster County on its list of the world's 100 most endangered sites.

local officials to review projected population growth and identify the most appropriate areas for future growth.

The strategy that emerged from this process is called *Landscapes: Managing Change in Chester County*. Designed to guide growth through 2020, it outlines four distinct types of landscape in the county: natural, rural, suburban, and urban. The plan sketches out a vision for what each type would be like in 2020, discusses the inevitable tradeoffs involved, and recommends actions—by government, the private sector, and local citizens—to make the vision a reality. These include, for example, open-space plans, farmland preservation programs, public infrastructure management, economic and community development assistance, and mixed-use zoning. The plan also establishes a framework for more specific subsequent plans addressing open space, watersheds, and transportation within the county.

One of the plan's cornerstones is an innovative feature borrowed from Oregon's tradition of growth management: to preserve and maintain the special characteristics of each type of landscape, it encourages local governments to establish growth boundaries, within which all future development will be concentrated. In implementing these boundaries, localities will literally be drawing the line against sprawl.

From Adoption to Implementation

Landscapes was adopted in July 1996. Now has come the bigger task, and the real test: implementing its recommendations at the local level.

Having made the creation of *Landscapes* such an inclusive process, the county has a reservoir of trust and goodwill to draw on. The implementation phase, too, has relied on collaboration. Its centerpiece is the Vision

Partnership Program, in which local officials agree to use *Landscapes* as a guide for their own planning efforts. In exchange, the county reviews local plans and ordinances and provides as much as $70,000 to fund changes needed to make these documents consistent with the county plan.

As of August 2000, 70 of Chester County's 73 municipalities had joined the Vision Partnership Program. The county planning department had performed consistency reviews for each member, to determine whether their plans and ordinances were in step with *Landscapes.* Through 1999, the county had funded 52 projects to update municipalities' plans, awarding more than $825,000 in grants.

To provide still more help, the county has published the *Community Planning Handbook: A Toolbox for Managing Change in Chester County,* which introduces a range of planning techniques, as well as sample ordinances, that local governments can use as models. The companion manual *Preserving Our Places: An Historic Preservation Manual for Chester County Communities* helps municipalities build historic preservation plans.

Chester County is also nearing completion of three functional plans called for in *Landscapes.* These plans will provide detailed strategies and recommendations to supplement *Landscapes's* broader policy recommendations. *Linking Landscapes,* a collaboration between the planning commission and the parks and recreation department, will present a vision for preserving open

Chester's award-winning vision.

"Sagebrush subdivision." "Coastal condomania." "The ravenous rampage of suburbia." In a 1973 speech, Oregon's governor, Tom McCall, used these colorful phrases to describe the threats posed by untrammeled growth. That year, under his leadership, the legislature adopted a statewide planning program that put Oregon in the vanguard of what we now call smart growth. In particular, the law required zoning changes to promote denser development, measures to reduce automobile dependence, and steps to protect natural resources. It also established state zoning for farms, ranges, and forest lands.

But the most famous element of Oregon's statewide growth-management framework is undoubtedly the urban growth boundary (UGB), a dividing line between areas where development is desired and where it is unwelcome. Under the program, each of Oregon's 241 incorporated cities was required to draw a UGB. Boundary areas include already-developed land, as well as enough undeveloped land to contain expected growth for 20 years. Two million of the state's 28 million acres are now inside UGBs.

Oregon's entire statewide program has been closely watched, but the city of Portland has received the most intense scrutiny. And no wonder: in metropolitan Portland, density actually increased between 1960 and 1990—an all-too-unusual feat for an urban area in the United States. In the same period, for example, density in metropolitan Atlanta dropped precipitously, from 3,122 to only 1,898 people per square mile.

Portland's accomplishment is all the more impressive in light of its population growth. From the early 1970s to the mid-1990s, Portland's population increased 50 percent, with only a 2 percent increase in its land base. What is happening outside the UGBs is equally impressive. About 40,000 square miles of Oregon's farmland and forest have been zoned to essentially prohibit development—an additional and powerful incentive to direct growth to where it belongs, inside the UGBs. Even near Portland, agriculture has continued to play a strong role: the two counties containing the western, eastern, and southern portions of the regional UGB rank second and fifth in agricultural production in the state.

Despite these accomplishments, Oregon's smart-growth laws are still not secure. In 2000, the state's voters passed an obscure ballot initiative designed to make local governments compensate landowners for the effects of regulation on property values. This measure, a radical departure from the more traditional and sensible rule that governments must compensate when their actions affect *ownership* of land, could bankrupt municipalities that adopt pollution-control and land-use measures, even those as simple as noise-abatement ordinances. As of this writing, the measure has been invalidated by a court order, but litigation continues, and the initiative's future remains clouded.

For now, at least, the old joke about Portland still holds: the difference between Portland and other American cities is that, with Portland, you know when you've left town. The quip reflects the city's—and the state's—great success in preserving its open spaces. Today, planning documents from across the country are peppered with phrases like "Oregon-style growth boundaries" and "Portland-style regional planning." Nearly 30 years after it was instituted, Oregon's statewide program remains a smart-growth model.[4]

space. *Connecting Landscapes* will be the county's comprehensive transportation plan. And *Watersheds* will present the Water Resources Authority's recommendations for protecting water quality and quantity.

Landscapes is a 25-year plan, so many years will pass before its full effects can be evaluated. History teaches us that, in land use planning, the best-laid plans do frequently fail in implementation. Still, Chester County's experience has already shown that different levels of government can come together, voluntarily, to promote smart growth. Its innovative approach has already attracted wide attention—and an Outstanding Planning Award from the American Planning Association. As other areas explore regional solutions to sprawl, they have an important model in Chester County and its commitment to education and cooperation.

COAST DAIRIES
SANTA CRUZ COUNTY

Visitors to the central California area known as Coast Dairies often imagine they have stepped back in time. The region, just five miles north of Santa Cruz, has changed surprisingly little in the last 150 years. It remains a quiet agricultural area, with 760 acres of farmland. Artichokes and brussels

PRISTINE CALIFORNIA COASTAL AREA SAVED FROM SPRAWL

sprouts grow where dairy farms once stood, and the tiny town of Davenport (population 200) is completely encircled by the property. Only two public roads run through it.

But, for a place with such a nineteenth-century feel, Coast Dairies has faced some decidedly twentieth-century dangers. In the 1970s, the menace was a proposed nuclear power plant. In the 1990s, it was sprawl. In response, local residents, environmental groups, and legislators banded together to keep the property free from the haphazard development that had marred so much of California's coast.

Island of Green

By the 1990s, 70 percent of California residents were living within an hour of the coast, and dramatic increases were projected for the state's population. Coast Dairies, the third-largest privately held piece of the California coast between San Francisco and the Mexican border, was a natural target for developers.

Yet it would be hard to imagine a place less appropriate for subdivisions or shopping malls. Coast Dairies boasts seven miles of coastline with beautiful, quiet beaches, and includes coastal dunes, chaparral, and three levels of ancient marine terraces. At 7,000 acres, the property is big enough to support a wide array of wildlife. Endangered steel-

Aerial view of the Coast Dairies farmland.

BUD MCCRARY

head and coho salmon swim its waters; mountain lions, foxes, bobcats, and deer roam its 700 acres of forest. In addition, Coast Dairies is part of a larger mosaic of open landscape in the Santa Cruz region, magnifying its importance still further. Residents knew that to save it, they would have to buy it.

Green pastures protected from sprawl.

Swiss dairy farmers first came to this stretch of coast in the 1860s. At the turn of the twentieth century, two families formed the Coast Dairies and Land Company. By the 1920s, the owners had returned to Switzerland, but their heirs continued to lease the land to farmers and dairy operators. The dairies closed in the 1950s, but farming continued.

Responding to the Threat of Development

While tenant farmers continued to live and work on the property, many potential buyers eyed Coast Dairies. In the 1970s, the Pacific Gas and Electric Company held an option on the property, where it intended to build a nuclear power plant. The company abandoned its plans because of the potential for a major earthquake. In 1993, the California Coastal Conservancy, a state agency, secured an option on the property and it seemed that preservation would win the day. But that hope was dashed the next year, after a statewide parks bond measure failed, leaving the Conservancy with insufficient funds to complete the purchase. Coast Dairies went back on the market.

SMART-GROWTH FEATURES

▶ Scenic coastline protected
▶ Traditional farming activities safeguarded
▶ Public recreational opportunities preserved
▶ Wildlife habitat saved
▶ Intergovernmental cooperation

In 1995, a development company based in Las Vegas, Nevada, acquired an option on Coast Dairies and made several attempts to develop it. By 1997, the company was poised to divide the property into 139 parcels for luxury homes, hotels, and a golf course.

Concerned citizens went to work. The nonprofit Save-the-Redwoods League approached the developer about taking over the option.

It also began looking for funding to make the purchase happen. The timing was perfect: the David and Lucile Packard Foundation was just launching Conserving California Landscapes, a five-year program to protect the state's natural resources, and it decided to make Coast Dairies its first project. The foundation awarded a major grant that enabled Save-the-Redwoods to secure the option. Other donors stepped in, and the purchase price—$43 million—came into reach.

But public funding was still needed. That funding had two eloquent advocates in State Senator Bruce McPherson and Assemblyman

SNAPSHOT: **SMART GROWTH AND WILDLIFE**

Poorly planned sprawl development creates fragmented ecosystems. They then can no longer support the most imperiled wildlife species, which require large, undisturbed areas. Instead, scattered development leaves only smaller, more isolated patches suited mainly for generalist species that are already abundant. The effects are cumulative and worsen over time. Thus, although the United States has enjoyed success through the federal Endangered Species Act and other efforts at meeting the needs of certain high-profile species in certain locations, we are witnessing a slow decline of others, especially songbirds and amphibians.

Research for the Biological Resources Division of the U.S. Geological Survey reports that 27 ecosystem types have declined by an alarming 98 percent or more since European settlement of North America. The Nature Conservancy, in a comprehensive assessment of some 20,000 species of plants and animals native to the United States, reports that current extinction rates are conservatively estimated to be at least 10,000 times greater than background levels, largely because of habitat degradation and destruction.

The effects have been felt throughout the country. California, for example, is estimated to have lost 91 percent of its original wetland resource, and 6 other states—Illinois, Indiana, Iowa, Kentucky, Missouri, and Ohio—have also lost more than 80 percent of their original wetlands. Dryland habitat is under siege, too: in fast-developing Florida, 15 of the state's upland-community ecosystem types are said to be imperiled, some critically; in Pennsylvania, the Pocono till barrens and serpentine barrens, which hold that state's two largest concentrations of land-based endangered species, are now under severe threat because they are being opened to suburban development. Quantified research by the National Wildlife Federation identifies sprawl as the leading cause of overall species imperilment in California, contributing to the decline of 188 of the 286 California species listed as threatened or endangered under the Endangered Species Act.

Smart-growth strategies minimize the impacts of development on wildlife. Smart growth encourages communities and states to assess and protect their most valuable habitats from haphazard sprawl, while also directing development to areas that are best able to absorb it and making more efficient use of land in order to take pressure off of currently open and natural areas.[5]

Fred Keely, both of Santa Cruz. The California Coastal Conservancy had already allocated $1 million in public funds to the purchase. McPherson and Keely pressed the state to contribute an additional $5 million, the amount that would close the gap and make the Coast Dairies purchase possible. Thanks largely to their efforts, the money was set aside from the state budget.

In early 1998, Save-the-Redwoods transferred its option on Coast Dairies to the Trust for Public Land. On October 26, the trust bought the property, ensuring that Coast Dairies would be permanently protected.

Planning Coast Dairies's Future

Securing the property was the first step. Next came deciding how to manage it—a complex, long-term process that is still under way. Some things are certain, though. Tenant farmers will be allowed to grow their crops, for instance, and public access to the beaches, which Coast Dairies's owners had always allowed, will continue.

The many other decisions that must go into the plan are now being hashed out by a diverse group: federal, state, and local governments; Save-the-Redwoods, the Trust for Public Land, and other environmental groups; and local citizens. The deadline for the plan is early 2002, and the groups hope to transfer the property to the government in 2003. Two agencies will take over responsibility for Coast Dairies: the federal Bureau of Land Management and the state parks department, both of which are actively involved in creating the management plan.

No matter what shape the final plan takes, Coast Dairies's future is now assured. Its nineteenth-century charms—and timeless natural values—will endure in the twenty-first century and beyond.

MONTGOMERY COUNTY AGRICULTURAL RESERVE

MONTGOMERY COUNTY, MARYLAND

Montgomery County, Maryland, which borders Washington, DC, is in many ways the quintessential suburban jurisdiction. Its central and southeastern sections, for example, have largely been consumed by the expanding Washington metropolis and contain all of the amenities—and many of the problems—that we associate with big-city suburbs.

THE COUNTRY'S LARGEST FARMLAND PROTECTION PROGRAM

But Montgomery is also home to something far less typical: the country's most successful farmland preservation program. The county's western and northern regions remain predominantly rural and, by and large, unchanged from earlier times. Here, family farms still dominate, with an average farm size of only 58 acres. Crop production is diversified, providing county residents with a variety of local products, as well as an important source of income—up to $23 million in annual total gross productivity. When hikers gaze down from the landmark Sugarloaf Mountain, their vision takes in a scenic array of gently rolling hills and rich farmland.

Warning Signals

This has not happened by accident. A careful observer in 1979, when the program was conceived, would have noticed signs of changing times: here and there, single lots and small subdivisions were creeping along the frontages of rural roads. A sprinkling of large mansions on five- to ten-acre lots dotted the landscape. Maybe the newcomers were attracted by the panoramic views of Sugarloaf Mountain, or by the charm of living in a working rural

Beautiful landscapes in Montgomery County.

GRANT DEHART

countryside within commuting distance of Washington. But their growing presence threatened to create a conflict between the county's traditional rural character and its increasingly suburban nature.

When such a conflict develops at the edge of a growing metropolitan area, agriculture is usually the loser. As the prospect of development drives

land prices higher, farmers' incentive to sell to developers intensifies. Property taxes may also rise dramatically, making it harder to eke out a profit from farming. In response to these pressures, some farms are turned into subdivisions, and general stores give way to big-box retailers. As suburbanization encroaches on the countryside, a feeling spreads among farmers that agriculture is doomed, and some begin to pull up root. Soon, the critical mass of farms and services necessary to sustain a viable agricultural community crumbles. To prevent this unraveling in its own agricultural sector, in 1980 Montgomery County launched an expanded agricultural preservation program.

Wedges and Corridors

Montgomery County has a history of thoughtful, pioneering land use policies. As early as 1964, the county adopted a planning policy called Wedges and Corridors, in which development would be concentrated along transportation corridors, while wedges of preserved open space would separate the developed areas. In 1973, to assure that its most productive open spaces were indeed saved from development, the county also adopted a Rural Zone (encompassing most of the western and northern agricultural areas), which required a minimum five-acre lot size. Unfortunately, this requirement did not deter suburban-style development of large-lot housing. In only six years, between 1973 and 1979, Montgomery County lost 12,268 acres of farmland, most of which was located in the Rural Zone. Clearly, a new, more restrictive approach was needed.

The County Council adopted a new master plan in 1980, limiting development to one dwelling per 25 acres in what it called the Agricultural Reserve. The reserve expanded the boundaries of the Rural Zone, from 80,000 to approximately 93,000 acres, to encompass much of the county's remaining contiguous farmland and rural open spaces.

Downzoning (requiring larger parcels for each new house) lowers land prices, especially in areas such as Montgomery County, where land prices had already risen beyond their agricultural value. With the possibility of less subdivision, the speculative value of farmland decreases. Thus, landowners in the Agricultural Reserve would have suffered an economic blow with the more restrictive zoning—and thus would have strongly opposed it—without a mechanism for compensation. This mechanism, adopted in the 1979 master plan, was the Transferable Development Rights (TDR) system.

Although, with a few exceptions, properties in the Agricultural Reserve cannot be developed at more than one dwelling per 25 acres, under the TDR system landowners retain "development rights" at one dwelling per five acres that can be used elsewhere—in what are called Receiving Areas. They can sell the excess development rights—and thus recoup their losses—to developers interested in building at densities higher than otherwise allowed, in other parts of Montgomery County. TDR Receiving Areas must be designated by the County Planning Board and Council and conform to local master plans. They are generally located where more development is seen as appropriate: where schools, roads, and utilities are already in place, or along major transportation corridors.

PROJECT DATA

▶ 317,000 acres total land in county
▶ 800,000 living in county
▶ More than 90,000 acres legally protected from non-farm development

As of this writing, 20 years after the program started, more than 40,000 acres of farmland have been preserved in perpetuity through TDR transfers in Montgomery County. (Whenever TDRs are sold, they are permanently removed from the property.) Although their market consists only of the receiving areas designated by the county, the TDRs are valued and sold in an open market without government interference.

Approximately 10,000 additional acres of farmland have been kept in agricultural production through county and state conservation easement programs that allow farmers to voluntarily limit development on their property. Conservation easements also stay with the property in perpetuity, safeguarding working farms and open space from any future development activity. The easements, which are spelled out in legal contracts, may also require the implementation of certain land management practices, such as soil and water conservation plans.

Why would a farming family voluntarily give up its right to develop its land, and follow required land management practices? Beyond senti-

168   SOLVING SPRAWL

While the U.S. continues to enjoy the appearance of abundant farmland, the best of that land is being lost at an amazing rate. At the conclusion of exhaustive research on the subject, the American Farmland Trust (AFT) reported that from 1982 to 1992 we lost to urban and suburban development an average of 400,000 acres per year of "prime" farmland, the land with the best soils and climate for growing crops. This translates to a loss of 45.7 acres per hour, every single day. During that same period, we lost an additional 26,600 acres per year—three more acres per hour, every single day—of "unique" farmland, used for growing rare and specialty crops. Put another way, for each acre of prime or unique farmland that is being saved by various farmland protection programs across the county, three acres are lost to development.

To make matters worse, most of the country's prime farmland is located within the suburban and exurban counties of metropolitan areas. Such "urban-influenced" counties currently produce more than half the total value of U.S. farm production; their average annual production value per acre is some 2.7 times that of other U.S. counties. Yet, ominously, their population growth is also disproportionately high, over twice the national average. Counties with prime and unique farmland found by the Farmland Trust to be threatened by particularly high rates of current development collectively produce some 79 percent of our nation's fruit, 69 percent of our vegetables, 52 percent of our dairy products, and over one-fourth of our meat and grains.

Smart growth helps contain these trends. In California's Central Valley, for example, the Farmland Trust found that doubling the average density of new growth from three to a moderate six households per acre could save some 561,000 acres of the nation's most productive and threatened farmland and shrink the "zone of conflict" between urban and rural areas from 2.5 to 1.6 million acres. It also could save some $26 billion in direct sales of agricultural products, as well as an additional $41 billion in impacts to agricultural support businesses, by 2040.

Saving farmland produces other economic benefits, too. Additional research by AFT and others has found that, unlike residential development, farmland produces a net surplus in tax revenues for local governments, because service costs are lower.[6]

mental reasons, such as wanting to keep the family farm as a working farm, it makes good economic sense. Selling conservation easements to the county on a 150-acre farm, for example, may generate as much as $400,000 outright—a substantial sum for farmers, who often run into liquidity problems. There are tax benefits too. (These are, of course, much larger for those who choose to donate the easements.) And the conservation measures and land management practices, while conferring environmental benefits, can also lead to better yields.

Government Bureaucrats: the Farmer's Friends?

Although conservation easements offer economic benefits, farmers might still be hesitant to approach a government agency that they did not trust. They might worry about unreasonable requirements, extensive paperwork, or too much meddling in their affairs. They might fear losing control over their most prized possession, their land.

In Montgomery County, farmland preservation programs are not run by the planning or environmental agencies. Rather, it is the Agricultural Services Division of the Department of Economic Development that oversees both traditional agricultural economic assistance—such as drought relief—and the county's conservation easement programs. In addition, the department also acts as a clearinghouse for the state easement programs. This way, a farmer can do "one-stop shopping" and compare the multiple state and local easement programs.

Since they are in the business of promoting and safeguarding agriculture, the department's staff members speak the farmers' language, know the economics of agriculture, and are familiar figures in the farming community. As a result, many farmers have come to trust the agency. "We do things to help our farmers," says John Zawitoski, director of planning and promotion. "We may even take their side when they are dealing with another arm of the government, and act as their advocates."

Landscapes and a Way of Life Saved

Over the last 20 years, large tracts of rural areas around the Washington, DC, metropolitan area have fallen victim to an unprecedented rate of suburban and exurban development. Counties that have not

PRINCIPALS

Public sector: Agricultural Services Division, Montgomery County Department of Economic Development; Montgomery County Planning Board

taken strong preventive measures to protect farms and open space have gone through a profound change of character. Loudoun County, Virginia, for example, long known as serene horse country, is now under severe threat from a traffic-choked series of new subdivisions. The nation's third-fastest-grow-

An often-voiced criticism of smart growth through land preservation is that it causes a shortage of affordable housing. If certain areas are off-limits for growth, the argument goes, then the supply of housing is squeezed and, given enough demand, housing prices skyrocket. This argument is hotly disputed by research indicating that land preservation has little if any effect on housing costs. In fact, housing affordability seems much more affected by unrelated factors, and jurisdictions without growth constraints suffer the same or worse affordability problems than those with them.[7]

Montgomery County has taken additional steps to assure that some of its housing stock remains affordable to those with low and moderate incomes. In particular, the County passed the country's first mandatory, inclusionary zoning law in 1974. The so-called moderately priced dwelling unit (MPDU) ordinance required builders to include a percentage of affordable housing in most subdivisions of 50 units or more (from 12.5 percent to 15 percent of the total). Two-thirds of the MPDUs are reserved for moderate-income families whose incomes are 65 percent of the area's median income; the remaining one-third must be offered to the county's public housing agency, to address the needs of the lowest-income county residents. In exchange for providing the affordable units, developers are allowed to increase the density of development by up to 22 percent over baseline levels, depending on the number of MPDUs provided.

By 1998, in less than 25 years, the program yielded over 10,000 MPDUs in more than 250 different subdivisions, at little cost to the county or developers. By the nature of the ordinance, the lower-income units are dispersed throughout the county's newer developments. They are often indistinguishable from market-rate units. In January 2001, the county executive announced plans to use financial incentives and county revenues to *double* the number of affordable units built in the county each year.[8]

ing county, Loudoun lost more than 20,000 acres of farmland in only ten years, between 1987 and 1997.

But, thanks to the forward-thinking policies of Montgomery County, most of the rural countryside in the Agricultural Reserve remains little-changed. Nature lovers still hike up Sugarloaf Mountain and enjoy views of an unspoiled countryside, or bicycle on quiet country lanes below. Children still delight in picking peaches and plums in the summer, and pumpkins at Halloween.

Meanwhile, farmers are adjusting to new market realities, but within a viable agricultural region. Some are shifting to flowers, sod, or specialty crops. "Agriculture has constantly been evolving," farmer Ben Allnut told *The Washington Post*.[9] Ben Allnut's father grew corn, but he plants fruits and vegetables that supply local supermarkets. The family has been farming near Seneca Creek for 200 years. Since the farm is within the Agricultural Reserve, Allnut can focus on the operation of his farm without worries about infringing suburban sprawl.

MOUNTAIN ISLAND LAKE

MECKLENBURG, GASTON, LINCOLN COUNTIES, NORTH CAROLINA

Neighbors have always treasured the beauty and serenity of Mountain Island Lake, a slender, 14-mile stretch of water in central North Carolina. The lake was created in 1924, when Duke Power Company dammed part of the Catawba River. It covers about 3,281 acres and has around

THREE COUNTIES PROTECT A PRISTINE SOURCE OF DRINKING WATER

60 miles of shoreline, home to rare flowers, white-tailed deer, red-tailed hawks, and many other forms of wildlife. Three counties border Mountain Island: Mecklenburg, home to Charlotte, North Carolina's largest city; Gaston, which includes the city of Gastonia; and Lincoln, which is largely rural, but experiencing increased growth.

The lake "is the crown jewel of the area," State Senator Fountain Odom once told the Trust for Public Land. "It is to us as Central Park is to Manhattan, only more so—it's not only our recreational oasis, but also the source of our drinking water."[10] In fact, the lake provides drinking water to more than half a million people—one-eighth of North Carolina's population. What's more, because the Catawba's sediment settles in a reservoir immediately upstream, the much-larger Lake Norman, Mountain Island's drinking water is of unusually high quality. In 1995, when Gastonia relocated its water intake from the polluted South Fork of the Catawba to the lake, the city's costs for chemical treatment were cut in half.

In recent years, rapid growth, particularly in the bustling Charlotte area, began to threaten Mountain Island Lake. Citizens feared that their tranquil, scenic lake would be overrun. Residents and government officials alike worried that new developments, located closer and closer to the shoreline, would threaten the lake's

The pristine waters of Mountain Island Lake.

water quality. To preserve the lake's character and the purity of its drinking water, they decided to protect key areas of the watershed from development.

Taking the Initiative to Protect the Lake

Mecklenburg County had already begun protecting land near the lake during the 1970s. For instance, the county purchased parkland and greenways through a $20 million bond package, and Charlotte-Mecklenburg Utilities began its own additional program of yearly land acquisitions. The county's parks and recreation department now manages those properties—totaling more than 2,700 acres—allowing only low-impact activities like canoeing, fishing, and hiking.

SMART-GROWTH FEATURES

▶ Unusually pure drinking water, serving half a million people, protected
▶ Sprawling development plans stopped
▶ Inter-county cooperation
▶ Strong local and political support for land acquisition

But nearly all of those efforts took place on the lake's east side. So, when developers began focusing on the Mountain Island Lake region, it was the west side they targeted. In fact, the west side was doubly vulnerable. It had many more acres of unprotected land; and there were fewer public resources available to buy and preserve property, since the region to the west was more rural than Mecklenburg County.

Realizing what was at stake, government officials, local citizens, and nonprofit groups from all three counties joined forces to create the Initiative for Mountain Island Lake. Spearheaded by the Catawba Lands Conservancy, the Community Foundation of Gaston County, the Foundation for the Carolinas, and the Trust for Public Land, the initiative set out to protect the lake and its drinking water by checking the spread of unwise development. To do this, it would raise funds to buy undeveloped lands important for water quality in the Mountain Island Lake watershed.

The initiative had an important government ally: the Clean Water Management Trust Fund, a statewide program—and the first of its type in the country—dedicated exclusively to protecting water quality. Created in 1996, the fund awards grants for land purchases and easements, distributing up to $30 million each year to state agencies, local governments, and nonprofit groups.

A major grant from the fund enabled the initiative to start off big, with an important acquisition on the lake's vulnerable western shore. In fall 1998, it paid $6.15 million to Crescent Resources, a subsidiary of Duke Energy, for 1,231 acres—six miles of lake frontage—in Gaston and Lincoln Counties. This purchase pushed the amount of shoreline within public ownership to 53 percent. The property will be managed as an educational state forest.

Developers Continue to Eye the Lakeshore

But developers kept their eyes on the remaining portions of unprotected lakeshore. Some of it, in fact, is already being built up. For instance, Crescent Resources has begun work on another Gaston County property, StoneWater, a development with more than 300 homes.

Fortunately, the Initiative has been able to protect other portions of Mountain Island's shore. A notable example is the property that almost became Water's Edge, an even bigger development proposed by the Provident Development Group, which would have been only 1,000 feet from Gastonia's new water intake. Provident did make some changes to its initial plans, in an attempt to minimize the environmental harm its development would cause. But local advocates remained concerned about pollution, erosion, and other threats, and they continued their efforts to keep the parcel undeveloped. For nearly a year, the Trust for Public Land negotiated with Provident for the property, reaching an initial agreement in June 1999. The fate of the negotiations, however, was up to Gastonia, since the town had to arrange the financial package required to complete the transition.

"Now is the time for bold leadership from this community," the Trust's regional director, W. Dale Allen, told the press.[11] Bold leadership was precisely what the Gastonia City Council provided, just a few days later. The council voted unanimously to buy and preserve Provident's 429-acre property and to issue up to $9.4 million in bonds for the purchase, to be repaid through a rate increase for Gastonia water and sewer customers. The sale took place in two phases and was completed in July 2000. The property is now protected by a conservation easement bought by the North Carolina Clean Water Management Trust Fund.

> **PROJECT DATA**
> ▶ About 45 miles—74 percent—of shoreline protected
> ▶ 4.2 miles of priority stream bank preserved
> ▶ Additional acquisitions ongoing

From Shore to Streams

Meanwhile, as it attended to the shoreline, the Initiative for Mountain Island Lake also looked farther afield. Protecting land on the water's edge would do little good to assure drinking water quality if the streams that fed the lake were not also protected. But which parts of the watershed were most sensitive and important to the goal?

To answer these questions, the Trust for Public Land contracted with the Carolinas Land Conservation Network (CLCN) to study the watershed. Researchers used a computerized mapping program that allowed them to look at the likely effects of variables including land ownership, development regulation, and the presence and size of wetlands. CLCN's report, released in 1998, identified 21 out of 127 stream miles, mostly in Mecklenburg County, as critical for maintaining Mountain Island Lake's purity.

Armed with this information, the initiative was better able to target its preservation efforts. It set a goal of preserving 80 percent of the remaining undeveloped, unprotected shoreline and the high-priority stream segments identified by the university study—all within two years.

Of course, funds had to be raised to meet this ambitious goal. Members of the initiative once again turned to the local government, this time asking Mecklenburg County commissioners to consider a bond act. The county agreed and placed the act on the ballot. Voters agreed too: in November 1999, they approved the $220 million Mecklenburg Land Purchase Bond. Fifteen million dollars of the bond would be used to acquire land for the initiative. A crucial new funding source was now in place.

The first purchase to draw on this new source, acquired in September 2000, was a 41-acre parcel that will be added to an existing nature preserve. In October, county commissioners approved the bond-funded purchase of land and conservation easements for another 344 acres, a transaction facilitated by the Catawba Lands Conservancy. And, in November, funding provided through the bond secured another 100 acres, a heavily wooded area that includes a mile of shoreline that will be managed by the county parks department.

The year 2000 was a busy time for the initiative: earlier in the year, the Trust for Public Land also secured 23 acres along a tributary in Gaston County, which will be managed by the North Carolina Forest

Service as part of the educational forest. Seventy-four percent of the shoreline—about 45 miles—has been protected since 1998. Progress has begun on the stream segments as well, with 4.2 miles of priority stream banks now permanently preserved. (Protecting streams is more complicated, since there are often two different landowners for a given segment, one for each bank.)

Through their votes and other actions, government officials and local citizens have shown their commitment to preserving open space in the watershed. Given the strength of this support, members of the initiative feel optimistic about acquiring more properties and assuring that Mountain Island Lake's exceptional drinking water quality stays that way.

MOUNTAINS TO
SOUND GREENWAY
SEATTLE TO THORP, WASHINGTON

East of Seattle rise the beautiful Cascade Mountains. Fifty miles from the city, Snoqualmie Pass cuts through these dramatic peaks. For centuries, Native Americans maintained a trail through the pass. That trail later

A GREENWAY CONNECTS SCENIC, HISTORIC, AND RECREATIONAL RESOURCES

became a wagon road, then a seasonal highway, and, finally, Interstate 90, Washington's main east-west highway.

A Highway Runs Through It

In the 1980s, I-90 was widened from four lanes to six. The 30-mile drive to Seattle from the Cascades, which used to take more than an hour, was shortened to less than 30 minutes. Seattle's suburbs had already been creeping east; now they mushroomed, with new homes and businesses seeming to sprout up overnight. People began commuting to the city from as far as 90 miles away. In 1990 alone, the Snoqualmie Pass route carried 43 tons of freight and 15 million people.

Rattlesnake Mountain towers above the greenway between Seattle and Thorp.

I-90 runs through a corridor of unusual environmental, scenic, and cultural richness. In the 100 miles east of Seattle and the Puget Sound, the highway passes through forests and parks, home to mountain lions and moose, herons and hawks, and spawning salmon—to name just a few of the many kinds of wildlife. Working farms and historic mining and logging towns dot its route. While some of these resources—particularly wildlife habitat—were irreparably damaged by the highway itself, they were now doubly threatened, as the highway began to spur land development.

In 1990, a group of hikers called attention to an idea for saving the wild and rural landscape on either side of I-90 with a protected greenway. On July 4, the hikers, led by Jack Hornung and fellow members of the Issaquah

Alps Trails Club, set out from Snoqualmie Pass on what they called the Mountains to Sound March, following their proposed route all the way to Seattle. Five days and 88 miles later, they reached Seattle's Waterfront Park. Their vision, the brainchild of Hornung, was a corridor of linked trails, farms, forests, and parks along the highway's route.

Creating a Green Corridor

It wasn't the first idea for a Seattle-area greenway. As early as the 1900s, the Olmsted brothers (sons of the legendary landscape architect Frederick Law Olmsted), who had helped plan the city's parks, suggested keeping the road to Snoqualmie undeveloped. But this time, the idea took hold. In, 1991, the year after the march, the Mountain to Sound Greenway Trust was created to help make it a reality.

The trust's goal was never to buy all the greenway properties, which would have been prohibitively expensive. Instead, the trust was designed to be a catalyst: it brokered purchases, when they were feasible, but it also facilitated land swaps with government agencies and press for environmentally and aesthetically sensitive uses of lands that stayed in private hands. It also acted as coordinator for the many public agencies and private landowners that controlled properties along the highway. Jim Ellis, the trust's chairman, once told the *Yakima Herald-Republic,* "There is no real power involved in the Mountains to Sound Greenway, just the logic of the ideas involved."[12]

The trust assembled an unusually diverse technical advisory board, whose members

> **SMART-GROWTH FEATURES**
> ▶ A 105-mile green corridor along scenic highway
> ▶ Scenic and natural values preserved
> ▶ Wildlife habitats protected
> ▶ Working farms, historic communities sustained
> ▶ Cooperation among government, business, nonprofit groups, and local citizens

included government officials and local residents, environmental leaders and forest company executives. They spent two years developing a plan for the greenway. Realizing that continued growth was inevitable, the board shaped a strategy that would encourage selected development in appropriate portions of the greenway area. As Bill Finnegan of Puget Power said, "People came to believe that development will occur, but with a good plan it can be controlled and screened."[13]

Since buying all the targeted lands was impossible, the board looked for ways to assure that private lands would be managed well. For instance, on tracts where logging occurred, it encouraged methods that would reduce environmental harm.

In the end, the Greenway Concept Plan proposed a 120-mile-long corridor from the eastern foothills of the Cascade Mountains, near the town of Cle Elum, through Snoqualmie Pass, to the shores of Puget Sound. At the time, other regions were also experimenting with greenways. But none matched the scale of Mountains to Sound.

The plan had equally ambitious goals. The greenway was designed to protect wildlife habitat, preserve the scenic beauty of the lands along I-90, and enhance recreational opportunities and tourism. It aimed to protect working farms and forests by allowing for sustainable economic use of these lands. And it set out to help the historic communities near I-90 retain their identities and sustain employment. All nine city and county jurisdictions along the greenway endorsed the plan.

A Vision Fulfilled

Today, the greenway is almost complete. It stretches from Seattle's Alki Point to the town of Thorp, 105 miles away. More than 50,000 acres of private farms, forests, and other green space have been protected.

The greenway has come together because so many parties were able to unite around the common goal of protecting open space. Support came from all levels of government. In 1993, for instance, King County and Washington State joined forces to buy 1,800 acres on Rattlesnake Mountain. More recently, in 2000, Senator Slade Gorton worked with Undersecretary of Agriculture Jim Lyons to secure a $10 million allocation in the federal Land and Water Conservation Fund to preserve 130 acres in the city of Snoqualmie. Meanwhile, hundreds of citizens have volunteered more than 60,000 hours to projects ranging from removing unsightly logging roads to maintaining trails. Corporate citizens, too, have played a substantial role, from paying for interpretive signs that now grace many of the trails to experimenting with new environmentally sensitive logging methods.

In July 2000, the second Mountains to Sound March took place. Hundreds of people participated, with 60 of them covering the full 130-mile course. Ten years after the first hike, participants were no longer publicizing an ambitious vision. They were celebrating a great accomplishment.

PEARL LAKE

ALMIRA TOWNSHIP, MICHIGAN

Many of the most celebrated open-space initiatives target large areas: extended stretches of river, long greenways, big urban parks, entire metropolitan regions. But small parcels are often worth saving as well. Sometimes they are home to surprising arrays of plant and animal life. Sometimes they connect broader expanses that need to stay intact in order to support wildlife. Or sometimes they are simply much-loved oases of beauty and calm. Pearl Lake, in northern Michigan, is all three.

GRASSROOTS, GOVERNMENT, AND ENVIRONMENTAL GROUPS SAVE A LOCAL TREASURE

Like the jewel it is named for, Pearl Lake is small, fragile, and extremely valuable. Located in Almira Township, 15 miles from Traverse City, the lake covers only about 600 acres. Yet this tiny body of water is home to a surprising abundance of plant life, as well as fish, turtles, snakes, and waterfowl. It is one of the few places in Michigan where threatened loons, bald eagles, and ospreys nest in combination. Moreover, its location—between Pere Marquette State Forest and property protected under an open space agreement with the state—adds to its importance. Pearl Lake is a vital link in a chain of undisturbed land. Together these pieces form a wildlife corridor for deer and other migrating animals.

Spring fed, with no major inlet or outlet, Pearl Lake cannot flush itself, so it is particularly vulnerable to contamination or disturbance. Until recently, neither posed much of a threat: Almira Township was a quiet, rural area (in 1990, only 1230 people lived there) and the lake and its surrounding wetlands were largely left in peace. In the 1990s, however, the township began to

Water and wilderness protected from development.

change. As in much of northern Michigan, the population grew and development increased.

Locals Take a Closer Look at Development

Residents had already become concerned about threats to the region's character and natural values when, in 1997, the McKeough Land Company of Grand Haven, Michigan, came on the scene. McKeough bought 251 acres along the lake's south shore, eventually announcing plans for a condominium development. At first, the company proposed 70 to 75 houses. The number later rose to 97.

Many of the lake's neighbors became alarmed, and a group of them formed Concerned Citizens of Pearl Lake. They hired an environmental lawyer, contacted wildlife and water quality officials, and worked with the media to publicize the proposed development. Another group of citizens, who lived farther from the lake, formed Save Pearl Lake. (The two groups later merged.) Together, they spent hundreds of hours on telephone calls, mailings, and other activities to raise awareness of threats to the lake.

> **SMART-GROWTH FEATURES**
> ▶ Vulnerable habitat protected from development
> ▶ Wildlife corridor safeguarded from fragmentation
> ▶ Undeveloped lake frontage added to state forest
> ▶ Cooperative approach among residents, nonprofit groups, government agencies

Those threats included construction runoff and debris, as well as sewage from the new houses, which would foul the lake's sensitive waters. The influx of new residents, along with an increase in boat traffic, would destroy habitat and drive away wildlife. Development would also fragment the wildlife corridor, harming deer and other animals that moved through the area.

Local officials were also worried about rapidly escalating sprawl. In response to McKeough's purchase, Almira Township enacted a ninety-day moratorium on development in order to review its land-use laws. Citizens and officials began working on new rules to manage growth and strengthen environmental safeguards, eventually drafting new regulations to protect sensitive areas better.

To its credit, McKeough tried to address many of the concerns. The company revised its plans to build houses directly on the lakeshore, proposing to move them inland instead. It also hired an environmental firm to research the impacts its development would have and explore ways to mitigate them. Still, local officials, the citizens groups, and the environmental experts they had enlisted all felt the lake was simply too fragile to withstand the proposed development. Pearl Lake needed protection—not only from the threat posed by McKeough's plan, but from future development proposals as well.

The presence of adjacent Pere Marquette State Forest offered a potential solution: if Pearl Lake could be absorbed by the forest, its 2,150 acres of lake frontage would be protected permanently. The concerned parties worked with a local land trust, the Grand Traverse Regional Land Conservancy. The conservancy approached McKeough about buying the Pearl Lake property, which it would then transfer to the state for incorporation into Pere Marquette. Meanwhile, the conservancy worked with the state to nominate the property for a grant from the Michigan Natural Resources Trust Fund.

Grants and Golf

McKeough, which had bought the land for $400,000, named its price: $1.35 million. In December 1998, after months of negotiation, that price came down—to $1.19 million—and the conservancy signed an option-to-buy agreement. Just a few days later, the Michigan Natural Resources Trust Fund stepped in. Agreeing with local advocates that state protection was the only way to shield Pearl Lake, the fund awarded $890,000 toward the purchase price. (The grant was one of six for land acquisitions in northwest Michigan, and one of 21—totaling $10.2 million—the trust made statewide.)

The remaining $300,000 had to come from private donations. Concerned Citizens and Save Pearl Lake, with help from other environmental and community supporters, met the challenge. They had already

raised substantial sums from philanthropic foundations and local residents. To fill the gap, they redoubled their efforts. How did they do it? However they could. They buttonholed neighbors. They distributed pledge cards. They held dances, bake sales, even a golf outing. The Pearl Lake Jamboree raised $3,300. An auction netted more than $20,000.

Their work was a testament to the power of grassroots activism. As Save Pearl Lake's Barry Harper says, it was "a fine example of what just a bunch of folks can accomplish, when enough of them decide to get together and do the right thing for their community."[14] It was an equally notable example of a community coming together and strengthening its ties. To save Pearl Lake, fifth-generation farmers worked with recent arrivals, forming friendships as they worked toward their shared goal.

All told, Concerned Citizens and Save Pearl Lake raised nearly $260,000 through their varied efforts to save the lake. Combined with the state's grant, as well as a contribution from the Grand Traverse Regional Land Conservancy, it was enough to make the periodic payments required by the agreement with McKeough. The final payment was made in April 1999. The conservancy transferred the property to the state in August, and it is now part of Pere Marquette State Forest.

In September, residents held a celebration at the southwest bay of Pearl Lake. About 60 people who had worked to preserve the lake were on hand. So, too, was one of the objects of their efforts: a bald eagle, which punctuated the ceremony by swooping across the water.

The Not-So-Impossible Dream

Make sure that when we change a place, the change agreed upon nurtures our growth as capable and responsible people while also protecting the natural environment and developing jobs and homes enough for all.
—Tony Hiss, *The Experience of Place*

When we wrote our last book on sprawling land development, *Once There Were Greenfields,* we noted that the story of sprawl was, in part, a story of the so-called American Dream of finding prosperity, a comfortable and convenient lifestyle, and a pleasant place to live. We noted that our story was about astonishing rates of growth and about progress and prosperity in our country, which, in our view, are good things.

But we also observed that the story of sprawl was about the dream's unanticipated twists. It was about patterns of haphazard development that had led to lost landscapes, congested traffic, polluted air and water, endangered public health, and a looming energy crisis that could make those of the 1970s seem mild by comparison. It was about how nearly all of the positive strides that we have taken in improving our

Preserved wetlands near Alexandria, Virginia.

environmental quality in recent decades could be reversed if we do not change the way we grow.

We noted that the story of sprawl was also about economic waste, rising taxes, and the unfair burdens that dumb growth places on taxpayers and governments. And it was about the consequences for those left behind as we have placed more and more of our investment and energy in new places—in our vanishing greenfields—rather than in the places where people already live.

As the stories in this volume demonstrate, however, the story of sprawl need not have a tragic ending. They illustrate that there is a better way, a path of smart growth that, if we choose it, can provide Americans with all the benefits of the American Dream, but without the accompanying nightmares. While the brighter dream of smart growth will not come quickly or easily, we believe now, as we observed then, that we *can* solve sprawl.

Few readers will be surprised to learn that there are those who disagree with us—who contend that the brighter dream we are pursuing is, at its core, an impossible dream. That those of us who are advocating smart growth are so many Don Quixotes tilting at windmills of consumer and business preferences that, despite what we may think, are not amenable to change; that attempting to solve sprawl is foolishly attempting to overcome destiny.

The stories in this book constitute our rebuttal to those who say that solving sprawl is an impossible dream. These stories make clear not only that sprawl can be solved, but also that America is clamoring to do just that. In fact, our biggest challenge in researching the book was narrowing down the hundreds of smart-growth success stories we found into a manageable and representative number.

Friendly front porches in Celebration, Florida.

As our examples also make clear, there is no magic answer, no single best approach to solving sprawl. Instead, there are many approaches, many incremental changes that we believe can collectively add up to a solution, to a more sustain-

SOLVING SPRAWL

able future. We hope readers are as inspired by these stories as we were when we found them. At a minimum, we hope readers will be motivated to conduct their own investigations and form their own conclusions about what we believe to be a fascinating subject.

New England farmland after a winter dusting.

Finally, we are honored to praise the men and women who are proving that the brighter American dream is not so impossible after all: the leaders, developers, investors, planners, architects, and citizens whose ideas and toil are showing us how to grow smartly. In the end, *Solving Sprawl* is not our book but theirs, and we are grateful for the opportunity to tell their stories.

Glossary

Adaptive Reuse

The reuse of older, functionally obsolete building or buildings. Often, the new use is different from the old—for example, an old warehouse is converted into lofts, or an abandoned mall into offices—and extensive retrofitting is necessary in addition to renovations. Nevertheless, adaptive reuse saves land elsewhere from development and usually confers significant energy and resource materials savings over demolition and new construction. In many cases, adaptive reuse is also the best means for economically viable historical preservation.

Brownfield

An abandoned parcel of land that is contaminated or suspected of being contaminated with toxic substances. Brownfield sites are often located in formerly industrial areas. Brownfield cleanup and redevelopment is important to the revitalization of many older cities and provides an attractive alternative to building on undisturbed sites. Obstacles include lack of reliable information of the parcel's history, cleanup costs, and determination of parties responsible for cleanup. Efforts are being made to overcome these obstacles at all levels of government, while communities and the private sector are becoming more savvy about the benefits of brownfield reclamation.

Charette

A planning session in which participants brainstorm and visualize solutions to a design issue. In the examples of smart growth we cite in this book, charettes have been used to help develop plans for entire communities or for particular parcels of land, and are frequently assisted by extensive use of maps, site plans, architectural renderings, models, or computer imagery. Charettes are usually led by a design team of architects and planners, although the development team, citizens, and public-sector representatives are often involved.

Cohousing

Housing that combines the autonomy of private dwellings with some aspects of common ownership and community living. Typically, each household has a private residence, but also shares extensive common facilities with the larger group. The development process is usually driven by future residents, not a developer: the housing is built according to residents' plans.

Comprehensive Plan

A forward-looking planning document for an entire community or jurisdiction. The plan is typically prepared by urban planners, but usually with extensive public input, including in some cases a final public referendum for its acceptance. Ideally, comprehensive plans help shape zoning and other local land-use policies, and decisions on individual projects are based on them. Not all localities have comprehensive plans, and many that do, unfortunately, cannot enforce them. Good comprehensive plans, even when not enforceable, can serve as important planning and organizing tools; when enforceable, they can set a community on a clear path and eliminate disjointed, piecemeal decision-making on individual development proposals. Comprehensive plans are often drawn up for twenty years, and may be updated every five years or so.

Conservation Easement

A technique that allows property owners to limit development on their property in perpetuity, usually in exchange for compensation of some sort. The owner signs a legal contract with a land trust or public agency to remove certain development rights (such as the right to subdivide, or build new structures) from the property. Conservation easements can be donated or sold; donations often result in large tax benefits for the owner. Property owners may choose to sell or donate a conservation easement for many reasons beside the economic benefits; for example, to protect a sensitive wildlife habitat for future generations, or to keep a family working farm from becoming a housing subdivision or a mall. Conservation easements may also require the implementation of certain land management practices, such as soil and water conservation plans.

Density

The number of housing units, people, or square feet per unit in an area, usually measured in acres.

Edge City

The term coined by writer Joel Garreau to describe large clusters of suburban developments characterized by unrelated high-rise buildings, parking lots, shopping malls, and large-lot housing subdivisions, without organization or governing structure. Garreau contends that edge cities contain all the functions of traditional cities but in a spread-out form. Yet few have come to recognize them for the new "cities" that they are.

Green Building or Green Design

Building design that yields environmental benefits, such as savings in energy, building materials, and water consumption, or reduced waste generation. Encouragingly, there is growing interest within the green-buildings community to add smart-growth location and features to the list of criteria for green buildings and developments.

Greenbelt

A ring of undeveloped or modestly developed land, usually consisting of farms, forests, and parks, surrounding a city or other developed area. If used strategically and on a large scale, a greenbelt can serve as a kind of *urban growth boundary* and successfully contain sprawl. If not strategic and large enough, however, greenbelts can unintentionally lead to leapfrog sprawl. Greenbelts also may provide recreational benefits and harbor wildlife.

Greenway

A corridor of undeveloped or modestly developed land. Can help to connect wildlife habitats and allow migration and movement of species. Also may be used for outdoor recreation.

Growth Management

A set of policies that guide where new development should and should not go, in some cases also guiding the pace of growth. Growth management policies can be local, regional, or statewide in scale, and regulatory or incentive-based in nature.

Infill Development

Development of a parcel of land that is surrounded by already developed areas. Unlike developments in sprawling locations, infill developments can make good use of already existing infrastructure, such as sewers, roads, public transit service, and schools, unless the existing systems do not have enough available capacity. Infill development reduces pressure to develop open spaces at or beyond a metropolitan region's edge.

Inner (or Inner-Ring) Suburbs

Communities adjacent or close to, but outside of, a central city. In larger metropolitan areas, older, close-in suburbs may form an inner ring of suburban communities between the central city and newer, farther-out developments. Inner-ring suburbs in older metropolitan areas are often linked to downtown by public transit and feature good pedestrian facilities, neighborhood amenities, and compact, efficient use of land. In spite of these attractive features, the outward migration of people and investments have left some inner-suburbs with urban-like distresses, such as declining housing values, deteriorating schools, and crime. Some are making a comeback; others never lost their popularity and continue to thrive.

Land Trust

A nonprofit organization that preserves and protects undeveloped or modestly developed land. Land trusts may acquire parcels from private owners by outright purchase or donation, or they may protect land by acquiring conservation easements or development rights. Land trusts also help land owners develop and carry out environmentally sensitive land management plans. Land trusts also often serve as intermediaries in complex land transactions; for example, they may temporarily acquire land and hold it for later acquisition by a state or federal park service or other public agency.

Live/Work Unit

A building or portion that contains both a residential and a work area (often, but not always, the living quarters are situated above the office/shop/studio). Since the same individual or family uses the living and working space, a live/work unit eliminates the commute. Such units also make efficient use of space and help bring daytime activity into residential neighborhoods.

Mixed-Income Housing

Generally, a development that contains a variety of housing types, sold or rented at significantly different prices. Sometimes the term is used to mean housing that contains both market-rate and subsidized units.

Mixed-Use Development

A development that contains two or more of the following, usually within walking distance: housing, offices, shops, restaurants, civic buildings, recreational and entertainment venues, schools, and parks. Mixed development can make for a lively, convenient neighborhood and obviate automobile use by giving people the freedom to walk, bicycle, or drive only very short distances to frequent destinations. Many mixed-use developments are also well-served by public transportation.

New Urbanism

Based on development patterns commonly used prior to World War II, New Urbanism is an architectural and design philosophy that seeks to reintegrate the components of modern life-housing, workplace, shopping and recreation-into compact, pedestrian-friendly neighborhoods served by public transit. New Urbanism also seeks regional coherence and preservation of open green space in metropolitan areas. (For more on new urbanist design principles, see "traditional neighborhood design," below, and the Congress for the New Urbanism, www.cnu.org.)

Pocket Park

A small neighborhood park.

Tax Increment Financing (TIF)

A public financing tool for a defined area's redevelopment that recycles increases in property, sales taxes, and other revenues from within the TIF district back into the district for a number of years (rather than allowing those revenues to go into the municipality's general fund). Typically used for more ambitious, larger-scale redevelopment projects, as these can yield a substantial increase in real estate values, sales and other taxes for the area. Often, the projected revenues allow public agencies to spend money on infrastructure improvements to the TIF district at the beginning of development.

Traditional Neighborhood Design (TND)

Design principles held by many New Urbanists (see "New Urbanism") to create neighborhoods similar to those commonly built in America prior to World War II. A typical set of detailed TND design guidelines might include the following: the scale is at the neighborhood level, which is to be no more than a quarter mile from center to edge; centers are to include public spaces, such as a square or public green, and prominently located public buildings; a vibrant mix of uses and a mix of incomes and housing types is encouraged; streets are to be interconnected (usually in a grid or modified grid) and pedestrian-friendly; public transit is to connect neighborhoods to each other and the surrounding region; open spaces, such as parks, playgrounds, and squares, are to be provided in convenient locations throughout the neighborhood.

Transfer of Development Rights (TDR)

A market-based tool for discouraging development in certain areas and encouraging it in others. In the area where conservation is preferable, property owners are given the option to sell some or all of their development rights (for example, the right to build a certain number of housing units on the property under current zoning regulations) to property owners or developers who can use them elsewhere, usually in designated "receiving areas" where more development is seen as desirable. TDR policies may contain additional incentives or regulations that encourage property owners in the giving area to limit development and to protect the receiving areas from overdevelopment. Whenever TDRs are sold, they are permanently removed from that particular property.

Transit-Oriented Development (TOD)

Development that puts people within easy walking distance of public transit service by clustering housing, shops, offices, and/or other functions within a short distance (usually a quarter of a mile) of a transit stop or station. TODs are especially effective in reducing automobile dependence when built around rapid-transit or light-rail stations.

Urban Growth Boundary (UGB)

A growth management tool that sets a clear limit to the area that can be developed within a metropolitan area. Inside the UGB, growth is encouraged; outside the line, growth is strictly limited. In effect, the UGB is designed to separate the urban and suburban areas from rural and open-space areas. To be effective, the location of a UGB has to be set very carefully: if it is too close in, the area within may experience stresses such as overdevelopment or a housing shortage; if it is set too far out, it may do little to contain sprawl. When drafted carefully and administered effectively, an urban growth boundary can be a powerful tool to contain sprawl and protect farms, forests, and natural areas from development.

Endnotes

Chapter 1

1 F. Kaid Benfield, Matthew D. Raimi, Donald D.T. Chen, *Once There Were Greenfields: How Urban Sprawl is Undermining America's Environment, Economy, and Social Fabric*, (New York: Natural Resources Defense Council, 1999).

Chapter 2

1 James Andrews, "Hospital Benefits: When Hospitals Close," *Planning*, December 2000, No. 12, Vol. 66, p. 14.

2 David Goldberg, "EPA Could Bridge Crucial Gap in Midtown Project," *Atlanta Journal-Constitution*, August 3, 1998, p. 01E.

3 Benfield, Raimi, Chen, pp. 29–88. Arthur C. Nelson, "Effects of Urban Containment on Housing Prices and Landowner Behavior," in *Land Lines* (Lincoln Institute of Land Policy, May 2000).

4 Christine Wicker, "Uptown: A Life in the City," *Dallas Morning News*, October 18, 1998, page 30A. "Neighborhood Bringing Lifeblood to the Heart of the City," *Dallas Morning News*, October 18, 1998, p. 30A.

5 Ibid.

6 "Uptown Living," *The Dallas Morning News*, April 21, 1996. p. 1A.

7 Charlene Prost, "Denver's Downtown Shows What Happens When a City Settles on a Redevelopment Plan and Surges Full Speed Ahead," *St. Louis Post-Dispatch*, October 31, 1999, p. B1.

8 Jay Walljasper, "When Activists Win: the Renaissance of Dudley St, Boston, Massachusetts," *The Nation*, March 3, 1997, p. 11.

9 1990 Census figures.

10 Walljasper, p. 11.

11 Benfield, Raimi, Chen, pp. 29–88.

12 Conservation Law Foundation, *The Smart Growth-Climate Change Connection*, 2000.

13 H.S. Lovato, "Art District Aspires to Become 'Soho' of Santa Fe." *The New Mexican*, May 29, 1995, p. B1.

14 Natural Resources Defense Council, "Environmental Characteristics of Smart Growth Neighborhoods: An Exploratory Case Study," October 2000.

15 Carl Nolte, "Suisun City Sheds its Seedy Image; Town Once Rated Worst Place to Live has Last Laugh," *San Francisco Chronicle*, September 3, 1999, p. A1.

16 Andrea Stone, "Community is Reborn by Going Back to its Roots," *USA Today*, December 27, 1996, p. 4A.

17 Bradley Inman, "'Let Suisun be Suisun;' Solano Town Went for a Unique Feel with its Downtown Revitalization," *The San Francisco Examiner*, May 28, 1995, p. E1.

Chapter 3

1 Sherry Jacobson, "Lofty Downtown Plans; Developer Envisions Neighborly Block of Apartments, Shops," *The Dallas Morning News*, February 19, 1999, p. 1K.

2 "Intown Living Comes to the Fore in Dallas, Atlanta and Houston; Quick Acceptance of Three Post Communities Shows Demand for Urban Lifestyle," *PR Newswire*, April 24, 2000, Sec. Financial News.

3 See *Greetings from Smart Growth America* (2000), a primer on smart growth produced by a coalition of sixty organizations promoting smart growth, <http://www.smartgrowthamerica.org>.

4 Jennifer Stern and Daphne Stein, "Irvington's Burnham Building is a Home at Last," *The Rivertowns Enterprise*, Friday, September 10, 1999, p. 1.

5 Timothy Egan, "Retail Darwinism Puts Old Malls in Jeopardy," *The New York Times*, January 1, 2000, p. 20.

6 John King, "Mountain View Mall Transformed to Cozy—-or Claustrophobic?—Mix of Houses, Condos and Parks," *San Francisco Chronicle*, April 22, 1999, p. E1.

7 Ibid.

8 See story on the website of the Sustainable Communities Network, <http://www.sustainable.org/casestudies/tennessee/TN_af_chattanooga.html>.

9 Benfield, Raimi, Chen, pp. 89–116.

10 Judy Hammond, "Less is More: An Architect Comes Up with a Winning Plan for Smaller Homes," *News & Record* (Greensboro, NC), August 24, 1999, Sec. Home Life, p. D1, (Knight Ridder News Service).

11 Jennifer Haupt, "Rooms with a Point of View—Clustered Whidbey Island Cottages Emphasize Community and Old-Fashioned Values," *The Seattle Times*, October 17, 1999, p. 26.

12 Ibid.

Chapter 4

1 Personal correspondence with Ted Harrison.

2 Ken Edelstein, "Keepers of the River," *Land and People*, Fall/Winter 1998, p. 2.

3 Dave Williams, "Barnes' Land Plan Spans State; 40 Counties Eligible for Greenspace Funding," *Florida Times-Union*, February 2, 2000, p. B-1.

4 For more information about Oregon's growth boundaries and other smart-growth practices, see the web site of the conservation group 1,000 Friends of Oregon, <http://www.friends.org>.

5 Benfield, Raimi, Chen, pp. 29–88. National Wildlife Federation, *Paving Paradise*, <http://www.nwf.org/smartgrowth>.

6 Benfield, Raimi, Chen, pp. 29–116 and pp. 137-160. American Farmland Trust, *Farming On the Edge: A New Look at the Importance and Vulnerability of Agriculture Near American Cities*, (Washington, D.C.: American Farmland Trust, 1994).

7 1,000 Friends of Oregon, "Myths and Facts about Oregon's Urban Growth Boundaries," November 1999, <http://www.Friends.org>.

8 Joyce B. Siegel, "Living With Affordable Housing," *Urban Land*, May 1999.

9 Stephen C. Fehr, "Montgomery's Line of Defense Against the Suburban Invasion," *The Washington Post*, March, 25, 1997, p. 1.

10 James R. Marshall, "Mountain Island Lake: Safeguarding a Pristine Reservoir" in *Building Green Infrastructure* (San Francisco: Trust for Public Land, 1999) pp 18–19.

11 "The Trust for Public Land Reaches Agreement to Purchase Water's Edge Property," PR Newswire, June 29, 1999.

12 In Joseph Rose, "The Interstate 90 Greenway: 110-mile Mountains to Sound Greenway Would Stretch from Elk Heights to Elliott Bay," *Yakima Herald-Republic*, August 15, 1993.

13 In "Greenway Plan Goes Public," *Mtns to Sound*, February 1994, p. 2.

14 Penny Misner, "Price of 'Pearl' Plummets, but It's Still Costly," *Benzie County Record Patriot*, December 23, 1998, p. 2.

About the Authors

F. Kaid Benfield is an environmental attorney and director of smart growth and transportation policy for the Natural Resources Defense Council in Washington, D.C. He has also served the organization as director of its land program, director of its forestry and agriculture projects, and legal affairs coordinator. Prior to coming to NRDC, Kaid worked at the U.S. Department of Justice and in private legal practice. He is a graduate of Emory University and Georgetown University Law Center and the author of numerous publications related to environmental law and policy, including the books *Once There Were Greenfields: How Urban Sprawl Is Undermining America's Environment, Economy and Social Fabric* (with Matthew D. Raimi and Donald D.T. Chen, NRDC, 1999) and *Reaping the Revenue Code: Why We Need Sensible Tax Reform for Sustainable Agriculture* (with Justin R. Ward and Anne E. Kinsinger, NRDC, 1989). He is a co-founder of the national coalition Smart Growth America and a member of several steering committees and boards relating to smart growth and transportation policy.

Jutka Terris is an urban planner living in Alexandria, Virginia. As this book was being researched and drafted, she worked on smart growth and transportation policy for the Natural Resources Defense Council in Washington, D.C. Prior to her work at NRDC, she was national field director for 20/20 Vision, a grassroots environmental and peace advocacy organization. Jutka also worked on urban environmental issues during service with AmeriCorps/Neighborhood Green Corps. She holds a joint masters degree in public policy and urban planning from the Kennedy School of Government at Harvard University and a B.A. in cultural anthropology from Grinnell College.

Nancy Vorsanger is a writer and editor living in New York City. As a staff member and consultant for NRDC and other nonprofit groups, she has produced magazine and web articles, books, and newsletters on environmental, educational, and criminal justice topics. Nancy has an M.A. from Columbia University and a B.A. from Williams College.

Parris N. Glendening is the governor of Maryland. He was educated at Florida State University, where he received a bachelor's degree in

1964, a master's degree in 1965, and a doctorate in political science in 1967. Following graduation, he joined the faculty of the University of Maryland, a position he held for twenty-seven years. His textbooks on government and politics have been used in more than 400 colleges. He has held numerous city and county offices and is now chairman of the National Governors' Association. In 1999 he received several awards for Maryland's nationally recognized smart-growth program, including the National Trust for Historic Preservation Honor Award and the Maryland Chapter of the American Planning Association's Outstanding Leadership Award.

Acknowledgments

This book would not have been possible without the support and encouragement of numerous friends. It is the collective vision and dedication of these wonderful people, institutions, and businesses that are, in fact, solving sprawl in communities across America.

First, none of NRDC's work on this issue would be possible without the generous financial assistance of the following supporters of our Smart Growth Program: The Nathan Cummings Foundation (for transportation-related issues), the Development, Community and Environment Division of the U.S. Environmental Protection Agency, The George Gund Foundation, The Joyce Foundation, The J.M. Kaplan Fund, Inc., Surdna Foundation, Inc., and our 500,000 individual members nationwide.

Thanks are also due to numerous colleagues at NRDC, beginning with NRDC's board and management. We would like to mention especially our organization's trustees Burks Lapham and Jonathan Rose, and our longtime friend David Hawkins, former director of NRDC's Air & Energy Program, now director of our Climate Center, and true renaissance man. We would never have gone far without the support and indulgence of Alan Metrick, our immensely talented director of communications, John Adams, our president and leader for three incredible decades, and, of course, our friend and executive director, Frances Beinecke.

A number of colleagues worked directly on the book with us, none more than Jessica Folkerts, who did everything from tireless research, to producing superb first drafts of sections to fill gaps in the manuscript, to managing the manuscript and its photographs, to making sure we authors did our jobs when and as we should, all with professionalism and competence that will continue to serve her career immensely. Jessica, the authors are in awe of you.

NRDC's reports manager, Emily Cousins, gave us her own invaluable professionalism and competence, even though entering the process midstream, and won our respect and gratitude while improving the product. There's nothing better than making a project more successful, and that's exactly what she did. Thanks also to Emily's colleagues in NRDC's communications department who assisted the project, including especially Rita Barol, Ian Wilker, Kathy Parrent, and Elliott Negin, who really should be a late-night disk jockey. We also thank our colleague in NRDC's development office, John

Steelman, for his support and friendship. Finally, we salute our former colleague Tanya Washington, whose good-natured diligence assisted this project in its early stages.

The community of people working on solving sprawl comprises an unusually gifted and hard-working group, who also happen to be the nicest bunch you would ever want to associate with. We must begin by mentioning our very close friend, as well as co-author of our previous book, *Once There Were Greenfields*, Don Chen, who gave us support and insight throughout the project. Dick Moe of the National Trust for Historic Preservation and Ralph Grossi of the American Farmland Trust continually give our work inspiration and counsel. And a number of friends in the community gave us their wisdom and advice after reviewing parts of the manuscript, including the following: Deron Lovaas, Sierra Club (now our colleague at NRDC); Elizabeth Humphrey, Maryland Office of Planning (now with Smart Growth America); Geoffrey Anderson, U.S. Environmental Protection Agency; our friend Lee Epstein, Chesapeake Bay Foundation; and Laura Watchman, Defenders of Wildlife.

Special thanks go to our friend and former colleague Matthew Raimi, who not only gave us thoughtful feedback on the manuscript, but also first conceived the idea of this book while he was at NRDC. We also thank Ed McMahon of the Conservation Fund and Roy Kienitz of the Surface Transportation Policy Project (now secretary of planning for the state of Maryland) for their advice and encouragement. And, of course, we thank our friend Constance Beaumont of the National Trust for Historic Preservation, and Doug Porter of the Growth Management Institute for allowing us to adapt their previous work on the Rutland Wal-Mart and Village Green case studies, respectively. And John Frece, Jesse Heier, Elizabeth Humphrey, and Harriet Tregoning for their coordination with Governor Glendening.

Turning to a very special category, this book was made possible because of the many wonderful people who gave us lengthy interviews and ongoing advice about the specific stories we tell. They provided us with materials and illustrations; reviewed drafts of the case studies; and patiently responded to a barrage of calls and e-mails with follow-up questions. We cannot thank them enough, but we can acknowledge them:

Addison Circle: Art Lomenick, Cathy Smith

Adidas Village: Jim Winkler, Bronson Graff, Janet Bebb, Mary Lou Munroe, Owen Clemens, Diane Dulkens

Antietam Battlefield: Grant Dehart

Atlantic Station: Geoff Anderson, Brian Leary

Barton Creek Wilderness Park: Valarie Bristol, Ted Harrison, George Cofer, Kathleen A. Blaha, Butch Smith

Bethesda Row: Nathan P. Fishkin, Cathy Hess, Richard E. Heapes, Bill Hausmann, Kristine Warner

Boulder's Growth-Control Initiatives: Melissa Schiff, Maggie Grise, Heidi Straszewski, Susan Ridgestone

Burnham Building: Jonathan Rose, Jeanne Johnson, Shelley Weintraub, Stephen McGabe

The Can Company: Katherine A. Hearn

Chattahoochee River National Recreation Area: Christopher D. Lancette, Slade Gleaton, Kevin Johnson, Helen O'Shea, Brett Busch, Kathleen A. Blaha

Chester County Comprehensive Plan: David Ward, Wayne Clapp, William H. Fulton

Coast Dairies: Lacey Tucker, Mary Menees, Darcy Rosenblack, Laura Perry

The Crossings: Joseph Scanga, Joe DiStefano, Lynnie Melena, Don Chen

Dallas Uptown: Art Lomenick, Cathy Smith

Denver Dry Goods: Chuck Perry, Jonathan Rose, Jeanne Johnson

Dudley Street Neighborhood Initiative: May Louie, Trish Settles

Eastgate Town Center: Rick Wood, Dorcas Perez, Joe Kohl

First Suburbs Consortium: Keith Benjamin, Ken Montlack, Ellen Burchill, Sam Brown, Gene Hix, Lydia Jackson

Mashpee Commons: Douglas S. Storrs, Nick Wheeler

MCI Center: Matt Williams, Seamus Houston, James E. McLaughlin, IV

Montgomery County Agricultural Reserve: John Zawitoski, Melissa Cunha Banach, Judy Daniel, Jeremy V. Criss, Grant Dehart

Mountain Island Lake: Bridgett Thompson, Bill Poole, Sarah Brunger, Kathleen A. Blaha, Gordon Smith

Mountains To Sound Greenway: Amy Brockhaus

Orenco Station: Mike Mehaffy, Rudy Kadlub, Debbie Raber, Arthur Mittman

Pearl Lake: Heather Rigney

Pulaski Station: Mary Nelson, Krista J. Kahle, Jacky Grimshaw, Carlo Ruth, Kevin Pierce

Quality Hill: Lillian R. Ryan, Tony Salazar

Reston Town Center: Randa R. Mendenhall, John Lovaas

Rutland Walmart: Constance Beaumont, Bob Rechner, Paul Bruhn

Second Street Studios: Wayne Nichols, Jonathan Rose, Jeanne Johnson, Ed Archuleta

Southside Park Cohousing: Pam Silva, Susan Scott, Mark Tavianini, Laurisa Elhai, Julie Osborn, David Mogavero, Renner Johnston, Pamela Wolfe-Konrad

Suisun City Redevelopment: Steven W. Baker, Martin Nelis

Third Street Cottages: Peggy Moe, Jim Soules, Ross Chapin, Susan Pelton, Pam Dotson

Village Green: Douglas R. Porter, Laura Deyarmin, Colleen Haggerty, Dana Vera

Westminster Place: Lillian R. Ryan, Tony Salazar

   Additional thanks go to: Dana Hall, Susan Otis, Ingrid M. Blanton, Rob Zako, Mary Kyle McCurdy, Randy Tucker, Scott Standish, Lori Paul, Christina R. Soto, Aubrey Harmon, Leann Little, and June L. Mengel.

   Finally, a very special thanks to Sharon Marsh for her encouragement, insight, indulgence, and support over the last two years.

F. Kaid Benfield
Jutka Terris
Nancy Vorsanger
May 2001